HOW TO GET INTO HEAVEN….
GUARANTEED

Shocking Statistics Reveals Over 95% Won't Make it into Heaven

Science Proves Who's God

HEAVEN'S AXIOMS

7

Required Steps to Insure You'll Spend Eternity in Heaven

How Religion Is Keeping You <u>Out</u> of Heaven

and
What You Can Do Before it's too Late

AL COLLINS

This book is for children to seniors and everyone in-between.

This book is especially for the billions in religious systems being deceived about how to get into Heaven.

According to God, every person has the opportunity to get into Heaven.

Accepting God's truth to get into Heaven… Guaranteed… is up to you.

All rights reserved. No part of this book may be reproduced or used in any form without written permission from the author.

Unless otherwise noted, all scripture quotations are taken from the Amplified Bible, Classic Edition AMPC

© 2024 Al Collins

ISBN Paperback 978-0-9997429-0-7
ISBN eBook 978-0-9997429-3-8

CONTENTS

SECTION 1

Introduction 9
Chapter 1 Some Uncomfortable Truths 21
Chapter 2 Is There a God or Gods? 25
Chapter 3 Science Proves There is a Creator and Who it Is 27
Chapter 4 Science and Jesus 34
Chapter 5 The Bible 40
Chapter 6 Science and Heaven 42
Chapter 7 Dimensional Crossovers 46

SECTION 2

Chapter 8 What Does This All Mean? 53
Chapter 9 The Second Death 56
Chapter 10 What's Heaven Like? 60
Chapter 11 WIIFM 64

SECTION 3

Chapter 12 What's Keeping You Out of Heaven 81
Chapter 13 Mongrelite "Churches", Ministries, Seminaries,
 Bible Colleges and Christian Universities 88
Chapter 14 Mongrel Leadership 104
Chapter 15 Mongrel Congregation, Laypeople, the Flock,
 Parishioners 138
Chapter 16 Religion Worse than Sin 145
Chapter 17 "Next" 152

SECTION 4

Chapter 18 The Stats on Religious Denominations.................. 161
Chapter 19 Infidels and Heretics.. 164
Chapter 20 Who Else Does God say won't get into Heaven? 175
Chapter 21 Can a Person Lose Salvation?................................. 181
Chapter 22 Sin... 195
Chapter 23 Forgiveness.. 203
Chapter 24 Blasphemy.. 209
Chapter 25 Prayer 216

HEAVEN'S AXIOMS

Axiom 1 Believe and Declare Jesus as Your Lord
and Savior.. 221
Axiom 2 Repent 228
Axiom 3 Water Baptism 236
Axiom 4 Forgive Others the Sins they've Committed
against You... 243
Axiom 5 Cease Heresy 244
Axiom 6 Cease Blasphemy 248
Axiom 7 Be Faithful Until Death... 249

Beyond Getting Into Heaven.. 253
Heaven's Treasure Map to The Meaning of Life 258
Afterword.. 269
A Mystery 274
Through the Eternities of the Eternities... 276
The True Meaning of Life 281
Supplemental Material... 283
Advanced Online Training 285

SECTION 1

Introduction

Good News, Bad News and Really Good News

THE GOOD NEWS is, you're going to live forever. The bad news is, doesn't look good for you at all if you're one of the 95%+ of the world's population that isn't getting into Heaven.

The really good news is, those in the <5% group will reign <u>with</u> God in Heaven through the eternities of the eternities.

So, what's keeping 95%+ from getting into Heaven?

Sin, unforgiveness, foolishness, ignorance, greed, pride, glory, arrogance, duplicity, indifference and fear are all to blame for this genocide of billions.

Then there's the butchers of the world (religious institutions, politicians, educational systems, corporations, media groups, etc.) that sell their insanity to all of us that will try and buy anything they peddle to obtain the true meaning of life.

Wikipedia uses a plethora of words, inquiries, expertise and perspectives like philosophical, scientific, theological and metaphysical in an attempt to explain it, before declaring that there's no definitive answer to the meaning of life or raison d'être... reason for being.

They proclaim it's whatever each person says it is for them but advise not to think about it too much as, "excessive pondering can be indicative of, or lead to, an existential crisis."

Makes life sound hopelessly random, according to experts.

The Meaning of Life

Does a definitive answer to such an important question exist?

Yes, it does.

For many decades, the meaning of life for me meant pursuing, scratching and clawing for pleasurable activities and wealth.

As placebos do, they eventually failed, prodding me to study and research history, religion, exercise, business and wealth in a futile effort to find the Holy Grail of the true meaning of life.

Everyone said they had the answers like "make more friends" or "do health and wellness my way" or "easy money with my new and improved process" or "buy this stuff" or "live in that country" or "this religion is the right one."

Looking for more serious answers I thought maybe doing "important projects" was the answer. Things "that mattered." Things that "make a difference."

Of course, these processes made only shallow, temporary dents into the realities of true peace, joy, love, contentment and fulfillment. I wasn't alone in this discovery as the rich and famous of the world, like actors, athletes and musicians were finding out the same thing. That fun and money and engaging in society's "dog and pony shows" isn't the meaning of life.

They're all carnival attractions with a fee. Once you get past the curtains, you discover that all their roads lead to dead ends. The unfortunate ones believe their illusions.

When I hit 40, I was struck with the, "you better wake up, you're not getting into Heaven," stick. It wasn't really a stick. It was a chilling knowing through my core that God's telling me, "You're a dead man walking."

I'd acquired and done the stuff that society and the world said was important, but as I looked around, I knew I'd been conned. It's not easy to admit to yourself at 40, or at any age, that you've been a fool.

The "church" Swamp

After God's stick event, I was thinking, "So, I have to go back to "church" now?" This wasn't a pleasant thought.

I'd grown up in a religious "church" doing all their Sunday school, worship services, confirmation classes, summer camps, shushing and genuflecting until I couldn't take it anymore and left when I was 16. They were nice people but laying it all out there I thought, "If this is what Heaven's like, I'm not interested." I couldn't imagine an eternity of what I was exposed to a few hours a week. My mistake was, I was equating religion with God. Another major mistake was that I blindly trusted them with my eternal life. I believed their false doctrines on how to get into Heaven. Had I died before I found out the truth, I wouldn't have gone to Heaven. I spent decades believing I was OK. With something as important as my eternal life I shouldn't have been so cavalier about verifying what I was being fed.

God shocked me by giving me a supernatural event (beyond a vision) of me stuck in a knee-high, muddy swamp full of thick weeds over my head. Every step I made was a struggle. I couldn't see how to get out. Finally, I saw an elevated grass hill to my right so I made my way to it. When I got onto the grass, I went up the hill to the top where there was a straight, paved road in both directions. The swamp was as far as I could see on either side of the road. I wondered, "What's this?" A voice spoke to me, "The swamp is the "church." Stay out of the swamp. Stay on the straight road."

For quite a while I didn't understand why God wanted me to stay out of "church." I thought I must have heard Him wrong. Why would God call "church" a swamp? It didn't take long to put 2 and 2 together to find out what happens when you go into and stay in that kind of swamp.

God's "swift destruction" on swamp leaders (2 Peter 2) is certainly justified for leading billions to their eternal deaths.

The swamp you're in doesn't matter, as the result's the same. Ultimate death.

When I say ultimate death, I don't mean physical death, as all the wealth, exercise, pills and doctors in the world can maybe delay your physical death, if a bus doesn't stomp on you later on today first.

Comeuppance

What I mean is what's called your second death. After physical death there's a comeuppance. Either reward or punishment.

There's an abundance of evidence available to discern reality from fiction when it comes to our existence. Truth isn't found in unscientific and unreasonable theories, ideologies, speculations and opinions.

Skeptics and scoffers who laugh at, ignore and even hate heretical, hypocritical, even violent religions are missing the true picture. Humanity's religions are failures. They aren't God. Consider yourself fortunate if you're not indoctrinated by some religious faction, however, being trapped in other irrational, illogical, dead-end chains of humanism, atheism and self-idolization is still imprisonment.

Don't make the foolish mistake I made believing that religion's concocted doctrines and its carnal leaders represent God.

What's in store for you now and in Heaven is beyond what you can imagine.

"But, on the contrary, as the Scripture says, What eye has not seen and ear has not heard and has not entered into the heart of man, [all that] God has prepared (made and keeps ready) for those who love Him [who hold Him in affectionate reverence, promptly obeying Him and gratefully recognizing the benefits He has bestowed]." 1 Corinthians 2:9

You're a special treasure of vital importance to God. Don't ever let anyone ever tell you anything different.

When I found the true meaning of life, I thought, "Why is the world and its governments and religious systems ignorantly and deliberately killing billions, including themselves with their lethal array of smoke and mirrors?" I also wondered, "Why are billions blindly believing the obvious death that these entities are shoveling?" Then I remembered, "Oh yeah, they suckered me too."

And who mentions the treasure? Seems like a given to tell everyone about the treasures. Even still, we're too mesmerized by the glittery junk treasures the world has to offer. This is why we need to carefully examine what we get ourselves into, especially in this case, as it pertains to our eternity.

Watch it

Long ago, God told Ezekiel to be a watchman on what happens to the righteous and to the wicked. How to live and how to die. God warned Ezekiel if he, knowing God's truth, didn't warn others, then he'd be responsible for their deaths.

I don't want anyone's blood on my hands so heed God or ignore Him at your peril.

"[1] And the word of the Lord came to me, saying,

[2] Son of man, speak to your people [the Israelite captives in Babylon] and say to them, When I bring the sword upon a land and the people of the land take a man from among them and make him their watchman,

[3] If when he sees the sword coming upon the land, he blows the trumpet and warns the people,

⁴ Then whoever hears the sound of the trumpet and does not take warning, and the sword comes and takes him away, his blood shall be upon his own head.

⁵ He heard the sound of the trumpet and did not take warning; his blood shall be upon himself. But he who takes warning shall save his life.

⁶ But if the watchman sees the sword coming and does not blow the trumpet and the people are not warned, and the sword comes and takes any one of them, he is taken away in and for his perversity and iniquity, but his blood will I require at the watchman's hand.

⁷ So you, son of man, I have made you a watchman for the house of Israel; therefore, hear the word at My mouth and give them warning from Me.

⁸ When I say to the wicked, O wicked man, you shall surely die, and you do not speak to warn the wicked from his way, that wicked man shall die in his perversity and iniquity, but his blood will I require at your hand.

⁹ But if you warn the wicked to turn from his evil way and he does not turn from his evil way, he shall die in his iniquity, but you will have saved your life.

¹⁰ And you, son of man, say to the house of Israel, thus you have said: Truly our transgressions and our sins are upon us, and we waste away because of them; how then can we live?

¹¹ Say to them, As I live, says the Lord God, I have no pleasure in the death of the wicked, but rather that the wicked turn from his way and live. Turn back, turn back from your evil ways, for why will you die, O house of Israel?

¹² And you, son of man, say to your people, The uprightness and justice of the [uncompromisingly] righteous shall not deliver him in the day of his transgression; and as for the wicked lawlessness of the wicked lawless, he shall not fall because of it in the day that he turns from his wickedness, neither shall the rigidly upright and just be able to live because of his past righteousness in the day that he sins and misses the mark [in keeping in harmony and right standing with God].

¹³ When I shall say to the [uncompromisingly] righteous that he shall surely live, and he trusts to his own righteousness [to save him] and commits iniquity (heinous sin), all his righteous deeds shall not be [seriously] remembered; but for his perversity and iniquity that he has committed he shall die.

¹⁴ Again, when I have said to the wicked, you shall surely die, if he turns from his sin and does that which is lawful and right—

¹⁵ If the wicked restores [what he took in] pledge, gives back what he had taken in robbery, walks in the statutes of life [right

relationship with God], without committing iniquity, he shall surely live; he shall not die.

[16] None of his sins that he has committed shall be [seriously] remembered against him; he has done that which is lawful and right; he shall surely live.

[17] Yet your people say, the way of the Lord is not perfect or even just; but as for them, it is their own way that is not perfect or even just.

[18] When the righteous turns back from his [uncompromising] righteousness and commits perverseness and iniquity, he shall even die in and because of it.

[19] But if the wicked turns back from his wickedness and does what is lawful and right, he shall live because of it.

[20] Yet you say, the way of the Lord is not perfect or [even] just. O you house of Israel, I will judge you, every one according to his own ways!" Ezekiel 33:1-20

It's up to you

Getting into Heaven... guaranteed, is up to you.

For all those who think they're smarter than God, He says, "³² For the foolish will be killed by their turning away. The trust that fools put in themselves will destroy them.

³³ But he who listens to me will live free from danger, and he will rest easy from the fear of what is sinful." Proverbs 1:32-33 NLV

CHAPTER 1
Some Uncomfortable Truths

STRANGE YET INTERESTING statistic says more people in the world believe in Heaven (69%) then believe in God or a higher spirit (60%). Makes one wonder where the God-deniers think Heaven came from.

This 69% of the world that believes in Heaven, think or hope that they're going there. But is belief in Heaven good enough to get you in? The answer is, no.

Doesn't everyone just die and that's it?

No.

Can the existence of Heaven be proven?

Yes.

Does just dying let everyone automatically into Heaven?

No.

Can I just think, feel, say and act however I want and still get into Heaven?

No, no, no and no.

Does belief in a creator or gods let you get into Heaven?

No.

Does being a member in a certain religion let you get into Heaven?

No.

Does praying a lot let you get into Heaven?

No.

Can someone else pray you into Heaven?

No.

Does hanging out with other Heaven-like-minded people in a building let you get into Heaven?

No.

Will owning or reading a holy book let you get into Heaven?

No.

Will praying to and revering physical things, people or even the dead let you get into Heaven?

No, no, no and no.

Will donating to or working for charitable causes let you buy your way into Heaven?

No and no.

Will being a good person let you get into Heaven?

No.

If you observe special days, follow the right religious person, wear the correct clothes, fast or eat certain foods, let you get into Heaven?

No, no, no, no and no.

Doesn't being pope or priest or nun or pastor or religious leader make a person special enough to get into Heaven?

No, no, no, no and no.

The reality is, anyone can make it into Heaven but most won't. Sad truth is, you're not getting into Heaven, unless you follow the required dos and don'ts for entry.

Whether you believe it or not, the reality is, each person is made of more than just a physical body (e.g. soul and spirit). You will always exist. After existence on Earth, you will exist either in Heaven or somewhere else… for eternity.

Therefore, making sure you'll get into Heaven is the most important decision you'll ever make in your life. Nothing else comes close to this decision.

Let's look at some truths, myths, lies, cons, deceptions, people, religion, the world and your decisions that are affecting your guarantee to get into Heaven.

CHAPTER 2
Is There a God or Gods?

People have diverging views on God and Heaven. They'll even go to war over it. To determine fact from fiction, does just blind faith-acceptance, conjecture or debating the doctrines of man-made religions and invented ideologies provide worthwhile answers, as each will say they are truth and others who disagree with them are deceived?

Name calling, shaking holy books at each other and even violence to verify a point doesn't prove a thing.

To obtain truth, people can look to various vehicles such as science and mathematics to back up or debunk any claims being made about a topic.

Despite what people say, we can do the same process with religion, creation and existence to logically determine and thus guarantee who the real God or gods is, if there is any, and, if there is a Heaven, how to get there.

Well-intentioned people say that faith is good enough for them to believe what they believe yet most people in the world have placed their faith blindly in ideologies that contradicts truth.

If science and mathematics fail to convince someone of the truth, then their stubborn, prideful, self-imposed prison will keep them living a lie and keep them from entering Heaven.

I've met numerous ones like this over my lifetime.

For this kind, supernatural acts of miracles, signs and wonders can be and have been successful vehicles in shaking them awake.

CHAPTER 3
Science Proves There is a Creator and Who it Is

D OES A CREATOR exist and if one or more do exist, how can we know who's who, as the world and its religions have created so many gods to choose from?

How can anyone know for sure? Isn't it all just opinions, theories, and a maze of religious "mumbo-jumbo?"

Rest at ease all who are skeptics or confused. Science has given us proof of the real creator God.

And science has proven not only that God exists, but also that the creator of the universe can only be... the God of the Bible.

There is also scientific proof of life outside of the physical realm.

Albert Einstein, theoretical physicist, Nobel Prize winner in physics, acknowledged, "the necessity for a beginning" and "the presence of a superior reasoning power."

Stephen Hawking, theoretical physicist, conceded, "It would be very difficult to explain why the universe should have begun in just this way, except as the act of God who intended to create beings like us."

Countless scientists over many decades from numerous countries have stated that no other conclusion is possible than a purposeful design using words such as, "somebody fine-tuned nature; super intellect; deliberately designed; overwhelming design; miraculous; hand of God; ultimate purpose; God's mind; exquisite order; very delicate balance; exceedingly ingenious; supernatural plan; and Supreme Being."

The Real God Disovered

The Astrophysicist, Dr. Hugh Ross, has given permission to quote from the in-depth research from his book, *The Creator and the Cosmos: How the Latest Scientific Discoveries Reveal God* (4th Edition RTBPress, 2018).

A very brief definition of an astrophysicist is a scientist with advanced knowledge of mathematics, laws of physics and astronomy who studys celestial bodies, such as stars, planets, and galaxies—the universe.

Dr. Ross, an atheist at the time, decided many decades ago to do an investigation of the holy books of the world's major religions. He said, "I figured if God, the Creator, was speaking through any of these books (I presumed He was not), then the communication would be noticeably distinct from what human beings write. I reasoned that if humans invented a religion, their message would contain errors and inconsistencies, but if the Creator communicated, his message would reflect his supernature. I chose history and science as good ways to test the revelation on which various religions are based."

In the world's holy books that Dr. Ross examined, he quickly found statements that were "… vague… clearly at odds with established history and science." They were religions invented by humans that "contain errors and inconsistencies."

He then tried to prove the Bible to be false as well. He "was amazed at the quantity of historical and scientific references and the detail in them." He set about to test the accuracy of all its statements. There was so much to check on that it took him eighteen months to complete his research.

Dr. Ross said, "At the end of the eighteen months, I had to admit to myself that I had been unsuccessful in finding a single provable error or contradiction. I was now convinced that the Bible was supernaturally accurate and thus supernaturally inspired. Its perfection could come only from the Creator Himself."

He said that the Bible stood alone from a perspective that went beyond the four dimensions that humans experience (length, width, height, and time). He said in *Beyond the Cosmos* (pg. 40-41) that his research proved that God "lives and operates in the equivalent of at least 11 dimensions of space and time. God can create space-time dimensions at will and is not limited by any of His created dimensions."

Mathematics and Laws of Physics Prove Who God Is

Dr. Ross conducted a mathematical exercise, "on the probability of the chance of fulfillment of just thirteen Bible predictions about specific people and their specific actions. My conservative estimate showed less than one chance in 10_{138} (the number ten with one hundred and thirty-eight zeros following) that such predictions would come true without supernatural intervention. That meant the Bible was 10_{58} (ten with fifty-eight zeros following) times more reliable than the second law of thermodynamics on just this one set of predictions. I also derived a similar conclusion based on the many instances in which the Bible accurately forecasted future scientific discoveries. All of the scientific and historical evidences I had collected deeply rooted my confidence in the veracity of the Bible and convinced me that the Creator had indeed communicated through this holy book."

That's on just 13 prophecies coming true. The Bible has had about 2000 prophecies fulfilled to the letter so far—no errors.

The atheist Dr. Ross said that he had no choice but to accept that the God of the Bible is the Creator and that He created us for a reason. Dr. Ross said, "I humbled myself before God, asking him to forgive me of my self-exaltation and all the offences resulting from it, and committed myself to follow his directives for my life."

There is much more evidence available than this research, regarding the universe and its designed creation, as well as about Earth and people. Dr. Ross studied different gases, minerals, planet, star, and galaxy formations and positions; archeology, history, and biological structures. More research than we can provide here. All of it pointed to God of the Bible as the Creator of all things. Including you.

Biology, Chemistry and God's DNA

The sciences of biology and chemistry have determined that the source that produced life must be an intelligent designer.

"The DNA molecule encodes information into alphabetic or digital form. Information always comes from an intelligence. If we trace information back to its source, we always come to a mind, not a material process." *Signature in the Cell* by Stephen C. Meyer

"Messages transmitted by DNA in the cell were specified by intelligence, and must have originated with an intelligent agent." Charles B. Thaxton, Ph.D., Physical Chemist

Genetic code, DNA, can be transferred when we touch something and/or through our breath.

The Bible tells us that God <u>spoke</u> everything into existence, <u>except us</u>. He <u>formed</u> us (transferred His DNA) with His hands and <u>breathed</u> His breath (transferred more of His DNA) into man.

"Then the Lord God formed man from the dust of the ground and breathed into his nostrils the breath or spirit of life, and man became a living being." Genesis 2:7

No other created being has God's DNA.

"So, God created man in His own image, in the image and likeness of God He created him; male and female He created them." Genesis 1:27

No other created being is in God's image and likeness.

You are part of the God species.

Archaeology and God

The science of archaeology conducted across Africa, Europe and the Middle East at 10's of thousands of excavated locations over hundreds of years has produced a mountainous collection of significant artifacts that has provided indisputable evidence validating the Bible as reliable and accurate.

These ongoing discoveries continue to demonstrate and support the authenticity of the Bible as the Word of God.

CHAPTER 4
Science and Jesus

SCIENTIFIC METHODS HAVE absolutely proven that there is a Creator of the universe and that this Creator is the same God of The Bible. God has 967 descriptive titles and names that are mentioned in the Bible. For our study we'll use the more commonly known name which is "God" and at times "Father," "Jesus" and "Holy Ghost, also referred to as the Holy Spirit."

Mathematical probabilities on certain fulfilled prophecies have proven with certainty that God had to have written the Bible (revealed to approximately 40 people over 1500 years).

"All Scripture is given by inspiration of God." 2 Timothy 3:16

So that means everything about Jesus in the Bible is 100% correct.

But, did science ever specifically examine Jesus to verify that He fulfilled prophecy?

Yes, they did. Actually, it happened many times by various scientists.

In one example, 600 University students were asked to examine just 8 of the 61 prophecies pointing to Jesus as the Messiah or Savior (some scholars say that there are over 300 prophecies that point to Jesus). The students calculated that the odds against one person fulfilling all eight prophecies are astronomical—one in ten to the 21st power (10_{21}). The American Scientific Association reviewed their analysis and found it to be sound, proper, and convincing (Peter Stoner, *Science Speaks*. Chicago, IL: Moody Press, 1958).

That was on just eight prophecies being fulfilled by one man.

The odds against one person fulfilling all 61 prophecies were examined by another mathematician. His estimate of those impossible odds was "one chance in a trillion, trillion, trillion, trillion, trillion, trillion, trillion, trillion, trillion, trillion, trillion, trillion" (Lee Strobel, *The Case for Faith, p. 262*. Grand Rapids, MI: Zondervan, 2000).

The Savior of humans that the Bible, history, and science point to is Jesus, also known as Christ; Messiah; Savior; Yeshua; Redeemer; Lamb of God; Prince of Peace; Immanuel; Son of God; Alpha and Omega and many, many more.

Who is Jesus?

This topic can fill many libraries. Jesus is God, along with Father and the Holy Spirit. When man and woman (Adam and Eve... refer to Genesis) sinned or disobeyed God they brought death (separation from God) upon themselves and the rest of humanity. Every person is born with sin DNA that's inherited, as well as sin that they do on their own. To avoid the second death (covered in Chapter 9), they must follow God's path to salvation in order to get into Heaven.

"Therefore, as sin came into the world through one man, and death as the result of sin, so death spread to all men, [no one being able to stop it or to escape its power] because all men sinned." Romans 5:12

"For just as [because of their union of nature] in Adam all people die, so also [by virtue of their union of nature] shall all in Christ be made alive." 1 Corinthians 15:22

Jesus came to earth, being born and raised as a human, to offer Himself as the only acceptable living sacrifice to die as an atonement or payment for the penalty for humanity's sin (among other things). All of them.

For a person to be absolved or pardoned by God of their sins they must accept that Jesus paid the penalty for their sins (accept Him as their Savior-more on that in the HEAVEN'S

AXIOMS). Only Jesus is the door to Heaven. Trying to enter Heaven any other way isn't acceptable by God.

Jesus said, "I am the Door; anyone who enters in through Me will be saved (will live). He will come in and he will go out [freely], and will find pasture." John 10:9

"Jesus said to him, I am the Way and the Truth and the Life; no one comes to the Father except by (through) Me." John 14:6

God is Infinite

God describes Himself in the Bible as being singular and plural at the same time-a Triune God-three Persons but one essence as Father God (Titus 2:13), Son/Jesus God (Hebrews 9:5) and the Holy Spirit (Matthew 28:19). Not a difficult concept for a Creator that fills and transcends at least 11 cosmic space-time dimensions. We are also triune as body, soul and spirit.

Human-invented theologies constrained by the limitations of human perspective confine themselves to four physical dimensions, such as Islam and Jehovah Witnesses, despite scientific evidence proving the God of the Bible is the Creator. Pantheism, atheism, Buddhism, Hinduism, and Darwinism are all scientifically proven to be failed belief systems (*The Creator and the Cosmos* pages 106-107, 121, 223-224).

Judaism is also a broken faith system as they refuse to accept scientific, historical and prophetic evidence of Jesus/Messiah/Christ/Son of God as their Savior.

Don't be deceived by others that sound good like the Church of Jesus Christ of Latter-Day Saints (Mormonism) and Christian Science. Wikipedia states that "relevant archaeological, historical and scientific facts are not consistent with the Book of Mormon being an ancient record of actual historical events." Mormons distort the deity of Jesus, among their other false doctrines. The Christian Science religion is neither Christian nor scientific, believing there's no such thing as sin to be saved from, among their other false doctrines.

"[22] Who is [such a] liar as he who denies that Jesus is the Christ (the Messiah)? He is the antichrist (the antagonist of Christ), who [habitually] denies and refuses to acknowledge the Father and the Son.

[23] No one who [habitually] denies (disowns) the Son even has the Father. Whoever confesses (acknowledges and has) the Son has the Father also." 1 John 2:22-23

"[8] If we say we have no sin [refusing to admit that we are sinners], we delude and lead ourselves astray, and the Truth [which the Gospel presents] is not in us [does not dwell in our hearts].

⁹ If we [freely] admit that we have sinned and confess our sins, He is faithful and just (true to His own nature and promises) and will forgive our sins [dismiss our lawlessness] and [continuously] cleanse us from all unrighteousness [everything not in conformity to His will in purpose, thought, and action].

¹⁰ If we say (claim) we have not sinned, we contradict His Word and make Him out to be false and a liar, and His Word is not in us [the divine message of the Gospel is not in our hearts]." 1 John 1:8-10

If you had weak or no faith or belief in God, or were following the wrong ideology, then root your confidence in the scientific and mathematical proof that the God of the Bible exists. He created everything including Heaven. He created you to have a special place with Him in Heaven, if you so choose.

CHAPTER 5
The Bible

THE BIBLE (THE BOOKS) is a collection of texts or books collectively called the Old Testament and the New Testament.

God directed about 40 authors over a span of 1500 years to write these 66 books.

"[16] Every Scripture is God-breathed (given by His inspiration) and profitable for instruction, for reproof and conviction of sin, for correction of error and discipline in obedience, [and] for training in righteousness (in holy living, in conformity to God's will in thought, purpose, and action),

[17] So that the man of God may be complete and proficient, well fitted and thoroughly equipped for every good work." 2 Timothy 3:16-17

There are more than 75 Bible verses that affirm that the universe had a beginning and that God created the universe.

THE BIBLE

The most read and widely distributed book in the world has over 3100 versions in over 2000 languages. However, reject and warn others of the watered down, flawed, altered and politically correct versions.

CHAPTER 6
Science and Heaven

God tells us in the Bible, His Book, that there is life after physical death for us, in Heaven with Him. Heaven is mentioned 703 times (AMPC) in the Bible indicating that Heaven exists as a place, not just in the mind as some religions proclaim. Science has proven the Bible to be accurate, so Heaven's existence is true. But, is there specific science and people's experiences to back up that there is life after death and Heaven?

Yes, again.

Near-Death or Actual-Death Experiences

Simply put, when we die, our soul (thoughts, memories) survives and leaves our physical body with our spirit. The most well-known examples of this reality are called near-death experiences (NDE), more accurately should be described as "actual-death experiences."

Dr. Bruce Greyson is considered to be one of the "fathers" of near-death studies. He is Professor Emeritus of Psychiatry and Neurobehavioral Science at the University of Virginia.

At a conference held by the United Nations, he describes documented cases of individuals who were clinically dead (showing no brain activity) but observing everything that was happening to them on the medical table below at the same time. He says, "there are cases that suggest that consciousness does not need a physical brain and in fact not even a physical body. It's unfortunate that just because we cannot explain something through materialistic means, it must be instantly discredited. The simple fact that 'consciousness' itself is a non-physical 'thing' is troubling for some scientists to comprehend, and as a result of it being non-material, they believe it cannot be studied by science."

It's not just a rare occurrence to be labeled a myth. NDE has happened to millions of people.

NDE Surveys

A Gallup poll, conducted in 1992, indicated that 13 million, or 5% of Americans have had a NDE. That's an extremely high number considering most people don't die on operating tables or from accidents and then return to life. A similar survey was also done in Germany in 2011, published by the Journal of Near-Death Studies, that found 4% had experienced an NDE.

People reported floating above their bodies and being shown a long tunnel with a light at the end. Some told the doctors and nurses what was going on in the operating room, down the hall or outside after they had been declared dead. Many went to Heaven and had talked with Jesus, angels, and deceased relatives before they returned to their dead bodies.

Many others experienced a place of torment, demonic torture, suffering, blackness and terror. When they returned to their bodies they were scared straight towards God, as they knew what was coming if they didn't.

A stunning book, *Placebo*, by Howard Pittman, reveals what he was shown in Heaven during his NDE and what God said to him. God told him, "Most people who go to "church" are in fact, playing. God said they don't have any 'light'." Pittman was shown "only two-and one-half percent going to Heaven. Ninety-seven-point five percent (97.5%) of those who died on Earth did not make it."

Other books have been written by people with NDE that can be searched for online, in addition to the availability of many YouTube testimonies.

The Reality of God and Heaven

Many people are searching for the truth. Few ever find it, as most accept different religions or feel-good philosophies to govern their lives.

Alternatives to God and His Bible have proven to be false. Be confident in the truth of the God of the Bible and His eternal Heaven for you.

"(And Ezra said], You are the Lord, You alone; You have made heaven, the heaven of heavens, with all their host, the earth, and all that is on it, the seas and all that is in them; and You preserve them all, and the hosts of heaven worship You." Nehemiah 9:6

"For it was in Him that all things were created, in heaven and on earth, things seen and things unseen, whether thrones, dominions, rulers, or authorities; all things were created and exist through Him [by His service, intervention] and in and for Him." Colossians 1:16

"And [further], You, Lord, did lay the foundation of the earth in the beginning, and the heavens are the works of Your hands." Hebrews 1:10

CHAPTER 7
Dimensional Crossovers

DIMENSIONAL CROSSOVERS WERE so prevalent in the Bible that we should consider them to be a normal part of life as well.

Angels

Throughout the Bible, Genesis to Revelation, numerous people were visited by angels or messengers from God that operate in multiple dimensions including into our physical realm.

"And the Angel of the Lord went forth, and slew 185,000 in the camp of the Assyrians; and when [the living] arose early in the morning, behold, all these were dead bodies." Isaiah 37:36

Visiting with God

People also visited into other dimensions, including this time eating and drinking with God,

"⁹ Then Moses went up, also Aaron, Nadab, and Abihu, and seventy of the elders of Israel,

¹⁰ and they saw the God of Israel. And there was under His feet as it were a paved work of sapphire stone, and it was like the very heavens in its clarity.

¹¹ But on the nobles of the children of Israel He did not lay His hand. So, they saw God, and they ate and drank." Exodus 24:9-11 NKJV

Further examples are in Ezekiel 8:3; 11:1; 2 Corinthians 12:2-4 and Revelation 17:3; 21:10.

This is definitely not limited to the Bible as numerous modern-day testimonies exist, including from myself. This is not astral projection. The misinformed and religious wrongly designate these experiences as witchcraft, which by their saying this, they not only admit a spiritual realm exists but their proclamation exposes them to blasphemy of the Holy Spirit (more on that later).

Ancient Miracles, Signs and Wonders

The Bible is a rich history covering thousands of years full of what we call miracles, signs and wonders.

Creation, angelic wars, sun standing still, fire from Heaven, instant healing and raising the dead are just a handful of examples.

Covering them all here would be exhaustive.

Modern Day Miracles, Signs and Wonders

Growing up in a religious "church" I was told that miracles, signs and wonders stopped in the Bible.

I thought, "How can God stop being God?" I was 12. I knew from reading the Bible that what I was being told was a lie.

How could miracles, signs and wonders stop, but I couldn't prove it as back then (1965) there was no internet or even books in the local village or school libraries to make my case?

Fast forward decades later I found lots of proof that I was right. "They" deliberately ignore all the proof out there.

Potent Evidence

I found thousands of people, after the Bible, who were continuing on with God's power. A few of the highlights you can look into are the following.

Desert Fathers and Mothers

The Desert Fathers and Mothers of the 3rd and 4th Centuries left the religious "church" system, same as I had, as they were disgusted by their heresy, hypocrisy, and greed.

They went out to live in caves and huts in the deserts of Arabia, Egypt, Lebanon, Palestine, Persia, and Syria. Many were illiterate.

Palladius, a roving reporter you could say, wrote a biography of his many years throughout Northern Africa, the Middle East and Europe living with and examining these numerous recluses, hermits, and ascetics, reporting on their stunning miracles, signs and wonders and dimensional crossovers.

Smith Wigglesworth

An early 20th Century Englishman plumber traveled the world for decades where cancers were healed, crippled walked, sight and hearing were restored, missing limbs grew, dead were raised and much, much more.

Maria Woodworth-Etter

A late 19th-early 20th Century American held tent meetings across America attracting up to 25,000 per night who received, witnessed and confirmed the same results as Wigglesworth. Threatened by her results, doctors at the time had her arrested for practicing medicine without a license. Newspapers savagely maligned her. Religious "churches" ruthlessly persecuted her. "They" don't like being exposed.

Lynn Collins

My main mentor, my mom, achieved similar results for many thousands in Canada and USA over a 35-year period. One of the last miracles through her was of a 50ish year-old man who was born with one leg shorter than the other. His leg grew out in an instant.

Dimensional crossovers are certainly beyond describable to witness and experience. Research them for yourself.

Don't allow the religious or the world's fanatics to sway you from the truth. They've been tried and found wanting.

SECTION 2

CHAPTER 8
What Does This All Mean?

Does this mean you have to stop following religions, philosophies and ideologies that don't proclaim God's truth in the Bible?

If you want to get into God's Heaven according to God's ways, you will. If not, you won't like the alternative.

Does this mean you have to become one of the "frozen chosen" by attending some religious "church" somewhere, anywhere, to go to Heaven.

No, it doesn't.

Actually, I advise against it. Remember the swamp testimony in the Introduction.

As I said, I was raised in a religious "church" (Lutheranism) that deliberately ignored a great deal of God's truth as well as accepted or turned a blind eye to what God says is unacceptable.

This rot can be found in all denominations that call themselves Christian.

Fake doctrines deceive billions, which has and continues to block people from entering Heaven.

"³ For the time is coming when [people] will not tolerate (endure) sound and wholesome instruction, but, having ears itching [for something pleasing and gratifying], they will gather to themselves one teacher after another to a considerable number, chosen to satisfy their own liking and to foster the errors they hold,

⁴ And will turn aside from hearing the truth and wander off into myths and man-made fictions." 2 Timothy 4:3-4

"If anyone comes to you and does not bring this doctrine [is disloyal to what Jesus Christ taught], do not receive him [do not accept him, do not welcome or admit him] into [your] house or bid him Godspeed or give him any encouragement." 2 John 1:10

Does this mean you have to become a hermit living in isolation somewhere or move to some third-world country to be a missionary?

No. Unless, God prepares you for that and it's your desire.

Many take action in some way on their own, thinking they're "doing good" yet encounter failure as they went without God. Jesus never did anything on His own. He always followed Father's will for His life.

Be sure you're getting into Heaven. Work with God from there.

CHAPTER 9
The Second Death

"It is a fearful (formidable and terrible) thing to incur the divine penalties and be cast into the hands of the living God!" Hebrews 10:31

The Bible records that there are those who will experience a second death, which is a spiritual or eternal death after their physical death.

"He who is able to hear, let him listen to and heed what the Spirit says to the assemblies (churches). He who overcomes (is victorious) shall in no way be injured by the second death." Revelation 2:11

"Blessed (happy, to be envied) and holy (spiritually whole, of unimpaired innocence and proved virtue) is the person who takes part (shares) in the first resurrection! Over them the second death exerts no power or authority, but they shall be ministers of God and of Christ (the Messiah), and they shall rule along with Him a thousand years." Revelation 20:6

"But as for the cowards and the ignoble and the contemptible and the cravenly lacking in courage and the cowardly submissive, and as for the unbelieving and faithless, and as for the depraved and defiled with abominations, and as for murderers and the lewd and adulterous and the practicers of magic arts and the idolaters (those who give supreme devotion to anyone or anything other than God) and all liars (those who knowingly convey untruth by word or deed)—[all of these shall have] their part in the lake that blazes with fire and brimstone. This is the second death." Revelation 21:8

The Bad Place

For the billions of people who don't accept truth or refuse to believe in God or Heaven, who follow their own philosophy of life, where does God say they'll end up if not Heaven?

Statistics say 58% of people believe in hell, mistakenly thinking and wrongly being taught, that hell is "the bad place."

That's another false doctrine. The Bible says those who don't get into Heaven end up in the lake of fire.

There are heretical denominations (e.g. Church of England/Anglican) that reject God's Word about the lake of fire, that is reserved for those who refuse God's offer of salvation through Jesus, falsely declaring instead that a person enters into a position of "total non-being" after physical death.

Some worship the devil or satan, thinking he, who God created, is as strong as God. Satanists also say everyone is annihilated or forever ends at their physical death. Science and mathematics prove they're wrong.

What does God say will happen to the devil, hell (hades) and those who followed a false way or rebelled against God?

"¹⁰ Then the devil who had led them astray [deceiving and seducing them] was hurled into the fiery lake of burning brimstone, where the beast and false prophet were; and they will be tormented day and night forever and ever (through the ages of the ages).

¹¹ Then I saw a great white throne and the One Who was seated upon it, from Whose presence and from the sight of Whose face earth and sky fled away, and no place was found for them.

¹² I [also] saw the dead, great and small; they stood before the throne, and books were opened. Then another book was opened, which is [the Book] of Life. And the dead were judged (sentenced) by what they had done [their whole way of feeling and acting, their aims and endeavors] in accordance with what was recorded in the books.

¹³ And the sea delivered up the dead who were in it, death and Hades (the state of death or disembodied existence) surrendered the dead in them, and all were tried and their cases

determined by what they had done [according to their motives, aims, and works].

¹⁴ Then death and Hades (the state of death or disembodied existence) were thrown into the lake of fire. This is the second death, the lake of fire.

¹⁵ And if anyone's [name] was not found recorded in the Book of Life, he was hurled into the lake of fire." Revelation 20:10-15

God says separation from Him, separation from Heaven and eternal torment await those who don't get into Heaven. He is truth. Every one of His promises are true. He doesn't lie.

"This was so that, by two unchangeable things [His promise and His oath] in which it is impossible for God ever to prove false or deceive us, we who have fled [to Him] for refuge might have mighty indwelling strength and strong encouragement to grasp and hold fast the hope appointed for us and set before [us]." Hebrews 6:18

Expecting no one wants that horrific second death result for eternity, let's examine what Heaven's like before we get to how you can get straight with God if you've been on the wrong path?

CHAPTER 10
What's Heaven Like?

PAUL, THE WRITER of many New Testament books, preferred to go to Heaven rather than stay here, "But I am hard pressed between the two. My yearning desire is to depart (to be free of this world, to set forth) and be with Christ, for that is far, far better." Philippians 1:23

People will give their thoughts, theories and personal opinions on this question but what does God say Heaven is like?

Jesus said, "[1] Let not your heart be troubled; you believe in God, believe also in Me.

[2] In My Father's house are many mansions; if it were not so, I would have told you. I go to prepare a place for you.

[3] And if I go and prepare a place for you, I will come again and receive you to Myself; that where I am, there you may be also." John 14:1-3 NKJV

"But, on the contrary, as the Scripture says, What eye has not seen and ear has not heard and has not entered into the heart of man, [all that] God has prepared (made and keeps ready) for those who love Him who hold Him in affectionate reverence, promptly obeying Him and gratefully recognizing the benefits He has bestowed]." 1 Corinthians 2:9

You'll find that reading the book of Matthew in the Bible will teach you much about Heaven.

The book of Revelation chapters 21 and 22 describe Heaven as streets of gold, gates of pearl, walls of precious stones, full of love, peace, joy, no more tears, no more pain, no more sorrow, no hate, no evil, no sin... eternal bliss.

Eventually all physical realms will be destroyed and replaced with new dimensions or realms where children of God will co-reign with God as His powerful kings, lords, saints and royal priests. How? Over what? We'll see.

"[1] Then I saw a new sky (heaven) and a new earth, for the former sky and the former earth had passed away (vanished), and there no longer existed any sea.

[2] And I saw the holy city, the new Jerusalem, descending out of heaven from God, all arrayed like a bride beautified and adorned for her husband;

³ Then I heard a mighty voice from the throne and I perceived its distinct words, saying, See! The abode of God is with men, and He will live (encamp, tent) among them; and they shall be His people, and God shall personally be with them and be their God.

⁴ God will wipe away every tear from their eyes; and death shall be no more, neither shall there be anguish (sorrow and mourning) nor grief nor pain any more, for the old conditions and the former order of things have passed away. Revelation 21:1-4

We will have new, indestructible, trans-dimensional bodies in Heaven that will be physically, emotionally, intellectually and spiritually perfect and satisfied. Never to experience pain, injury, sickness, weakness, loneliness, grief, depression or sorrow. No evil. Pure love and joy. Forever.

"⁴² So, it is with the resurrection of the dead. [The body] that is sown is perishable and decays, but [the body] that is resurrected is imperishable (immune to decay, immortal).

⁴³ It is sown in dishonor and humiliation; it is raised in honor and glory. It is sown in infirmity and weakness; it is resurrected in strength and endued with power.

⁴⁴ It is sown a natural (physical) body; it is raised a supernatural (a spiritual) body. [As surely as] there is a physical body, there is also a spiritual body." 1 Corinthians 15:42-44

"⁵⁰ But I tell you this, brethren, flesh and blood cannot [become partakers of eternal salvation and] inherit or share in the kingdom of God; nor does the perishable (that which is decaying) inherit or share in the imperishable (the immortal).

⁵¹ Take notice! I tell you a mystery (a secret truth, an event decreed by the hidden purpose or counsel of God). We shall not all fall asleep [in death], but we shall all be changed (transformed)

⁵² In a moment, in the twinkling of an eye, at the [sound of the] last trumpet call. For a trumpet will sound, and the dead [in Christ] will be raised imperishable (free and immune from decay), and we shall be changed (transformed).

⁵³ For this perishable [part of us] must put on the imperishable [nature], and this mortal [part of us, this nature that is capable of dying] must put on immortality (freedom from death).

⁵⁴ And when this perishable puts on the imperishable and this that was capable of dying puts on freedom from death, then shall be fulfilled the Scripture that says, Death is swallowed up (utterly vanquished forever) in and unto victory." 1 Corinthians 15:50-54

CHAPTER 11
WIIFM

WIIFM (WHAT'S IN IT FOR ME) you say about Heaven? Aside from avoiding the lake of fire, God has much instore for those who will get into Heaven.

"For the Lord God is a Sun and Shield; the Lord bestows [present] grace and favor and [future] glory (honor, splendor, and heavenly bliss)! No good thing will He withhold from those who walk uprightly." Psalm 84:11

Father is Pure Love… it is in His Nature to bless and reward His children.

Many people think when they die that they'll be floating around in Heaven somewhere, on a cloud plucking a harp. Oddly, many think that they will become angels when they die. As mentioned, many believe, in error, that everyone goes to Heaven. This thinking is the dead fruit of the false doctrines of man. God promises us <u>exactly</u> what we inherit <u>now</u>, as well as when we arrive in Heaven.

Titles

When we accept Jesus as our Lord and Savior, we immediately receive some new titles.

Citizen of Heaven

"But we are citizens of the state (commonwealth, homeland) which is in heaven." Philippians 3:20

Co-joined with God

"Anyone who confesses (acknowledges, owns) that Jesus is the Son of God, God abides (lives, makes His home) in him and he [abides, lives, makes his home] in God." 1 John 4:15

God

"I said, You are gods [since you judge on My behalf, as My representatives]; indeed, all of you are children of the Most High." Psalm 82:6

"Jesus answered, Is it not written in your Law, I said, You are gods?" John 10:34

Joint-Heir with Christ

"¹⁶ The Spirit Himself [thus] testifies together with our own spirit, [assuring us] that we are children of God.

¹⁷ And if we are [His] children, then we are [His] heirs also: heirs of God and fellow heirs with Christ [sharing His inheritance with Him]; only we must share His suffering if we are to share His glory." Romans 8:16-17

"And He raised us up together with Him and made us sit down together [giving us joint seating with Him] in the heavenly sphere [by virtue of our being] in Christ Jesus (the Messiah, the Anointed One)." Ephesians 2:6

Lord and King

"They will wage war against the Lamb, and the Lamb will triumph over them; for He is Lord of lords and King of kings—and those with Him and on His side are chosen and called [elected] and loyal and faithful followers." Revelation 17:14

New creation (beyond human)

"Therefore, if any person is [ingrafted] in Christ (the Messiah) he is a new creation (a new creature altogether); the old [previous moral and spiritual condition] has passed away. Behold, the fresh and new has come!" 2 Corinthians 5:17

"Therefore, you are no longer outsiders (exiles, migrants, and aliens, excluded from the rights of citizens), but you now share citizenship with the saints (God's own people, consecrated and set apart for Himself); and you belong to God's [own] household." Ephesians 2:19

Royal Priest

"But you are a chosen race, a royal priesthood, a dedicated nation, [God's] own purchased, special people, that you may set forth the wonderful deeds and display the virtues and perfections of Him Who called you out of darkness into His marvelous light." 1 Peter 2:9

Saint

"To those consecrated and purified and made holy in Christ Jesus, [who are] selected and called to be saints (God's people)." 1 Corinthians 1:2b

See also Psalm 31:23; Acts 9:13, 32: 26:10; Romans 8:27, 16:2; Ephesians 2:19, 4:12, 5:3, Philippians 4:21; Colossians 1:3-4, 11-13: Hebrews 6:10.

Son of light

"For you are all sons of light and sons of the day; we do not belong either to the night or to darkness." 1 Thessalonians 5:5

Son of the day "For you are all sons of light and sons of the day; we do not belong either to the night or to darkness." 1 Thessalonians 5:5

Temple of God

"Do you not discern and understand that you [the whole church at Corinth] are God's temple (His sanctuary), and that God's Spirit has His permanent dwelling in you [to be at home in you, collectively as a church and also individually]?" 1 Corinthians 3:16

See Romans 8 for more.

Condemnations and Rewards

In Revelation, Jesus is speaking to us about the seven assemblies made up of His followers in Chapters 2 and 3. His primary intention is to convey a "report card" for the assemblies of that time. The secondary purpose is to describe seven types of assemblies, and individual followers, throughout history. These short letters act as warnings and encouragement to those who call themselves, "followers of Christ."

The Ephesus Assembly

Condemnations

Despite looking good on the outside... persevering, working for the Master, "trying spirits," exposing false apostles, against evil, not giving up... the inside of this person is sick, as "that you have left (abandoned) the love that you had at first [you have deserted Me, your first love]" Revelation 2:4b. Their hearts are no longer on fire for the Lord Jesus Christ. This person has embraced religion... "These people draw near Me with their mouths and honor Me with their lips, but their hearts hold off and are far away from Me." Matthew 15:8

Rewards

To those who keep their first love (Jesus)... To him who overcomes (is victorious), I will grant to eat [of the fruit] of the tree of life, which is in the paradise of God." Revelation 2:7b

The Smyrna Assembly

Condemnations

None.

Rewards

To the Jesus follower that Conquers worldly wealth, persecution, trials, tribulations, is faithful unto death, will receive... "I will give you the crown of life" Revelation 2:10b <u>and</u> "He who overcomes (is victorious) shall in no way be injured by the second death" (lake of fire). Revelation 2:11b

The Pergamos Assembly

Condemnations

Accepts the doctrine of Baalam (idolatry and sexual immorality) and the doctrine of the Nicolaitanes (impure/immoral/false doctrines, adultery and fornication).

Rewards

"To him who overcomes (conquers), I will give to eat of the manna that is hidden, <u>and</u> I will give him a white stone with a new name engraved on the stone, which no one knows or understands except he who receives it" Revelation 2:17b

The Thyatira Assembly

Condemnations

Despite their good works, faith, patience, and charity, they allow a spirit of Jezebel to teach and seduce them and others to commit fornication and participate in idolatrous practices. Many are seduced by a dynamic personality and a slick presentation, which does not guarantee that they are teaching truth—some leaders and non-leaders knowingly and deliberately deceive others.

Rewards

"^{26} And he who overcomes (is victorious) and who obeys My commands to the [very] end [doing the works that please Me], I will give him authority and power over the nations;

^{27} And he shall rule them with a scepter (rod) of iron, as when earthen pots are broken in pieces, and [his power over them shall be] like that which I Myself have received from My Father;

^{28} And I will give him the Morning Star.

^{29} He who is able to hear, let him listen to and heed what the [Holy] Spirit says to the assemblies (churches)." Revelation 2:26-29

The Sardis Assembly

Condemnations

Reputation of being a "live" follower of God, but actually is spiritually dead, imperfect works and few remaining good qualities.

Rewards

"Thus, shall he who conquers (is victorious) be clad in white garments, and I will not erase or blot out his name from the Book of Life; I will acknowledge him [as Mine] and I will confess his name openly before My Father and before His angels." Revelation 3:5

The Philadelphia Assembly

Condemnations

None

Rewards

"He who overcomes (is victorious), I will make him a pillar in the sanctuary of My God; he shall never be put out of it or go out of it, and I will write on him the name of My God and the name of the city of My God, the new Jerusalem, which descends from My God out of heaven, and My own new name." Revelation 3:12

The Laodicea Assembly

Condemnations

Spiritually lukewarm… do-nothings, lovers of worldly material things and prosperity.

Rewards

"He who overcomes (is victorious), I will grant him to sit beside Me on My throne, as I Myself overcame (was victorious) and sat down beside My Father on His throne." Revelation 3:21

OK... sit down, get a firm grip on your chair and read this one again...

One of your rewards is... you will sit beside God on His throne.

As we can see by these 7 types of assemblies/individuals, anyone can <u>say</u> they're a follower of Jesus and the Bible, yet most will be condemned—most will <u>not</u> receive rewards.

Jesus promises that those who overcome will <u>definitely</u> receive these rewards.

Crowns

We also receive these crowns.

The Incorruptible Crown

"Know ye not that they which run in a race run all, but one receiveth the prize? So run, that ye may obtain. And every man that striveth for the mastery is temperate in all things. Now they do it to obtain a corruptible crown; but we an incorruptible." 1 Corinthians 9:25-27 KJV

The Crown of Rejoicing

"For what is our hope, or joy, or crown of rejoicing? Is it not even you in the presence of our Lord Jesus Christ at His coming?" 1 Thessalonians 2:19 NKJV

The Crown of Righteousness

"[As to what remains] henceforth there is laid up for me the [victor's] crown of righteousness [for being right with God and doing right], which the Lord, the righteous Judge, will award to me and recompense me on that [great] day—and not to me only, but also to all those who have loved and yearned for and welcomed His appearing (His return)." 2 Timothy 4:8

The Crown of Life

"Blessed (happy, to be envied) is the man who is patient under trial and stands up under temptation, for when he has stood the test and been approved, he will receive [the victor's] crown of life which God has promised to those who love Him." James 1:12

"Be loyally faithful unto death [even if you must die for it], and I will give you the crown of life." Revelation 2:10

The Crown of Glory

"And [then] when the Chief Shepherd is revealed, you will win the conqueror's crown of glory." 1 Peter 5:4

Crown of Anointing Oil

"Neither shall he go out of the sanctuary nor desecrate or make ceremonially unclean the sanctuary of his God, for the crown or consecration of the anointing oil of his God is upon him. I am the Lord." Leviticus 21:12

And of course we receive the following wonderful gifts as well.

Love

"And we know (understand, recognize, are conscious of, by observation and by experience) and believe (adhere to and put faith in and rely on) the love God cherishes for us. God is love, and he who dwells and continues in love dwells and continues in God, and God dwells and continues in him." 1 John 4:16

Joy

"You will show me the path of life; in Your presence is fullness of joy, at Your right hand there are pleasures forevermore." Psalm 16:11

Peace

"Now may the Lord of peace Himself grant you His peace (the peace of His kingdom) at all times and in all ways [under all circumstances and conditions, whatever comes]. The Lord [be] with you all." 2 Thessalonians 3:16

How does anything the world has to offer come close to any of that for the meaning of life?

Jesus said in Matthew 6:33, "But seek (aim at and strive after) first of all His kingdom and His righteousness (His way of doing and being right), and then all these things taken together will be given you besides."

"9 For we are fellow workmen (joint promoters, laborers together) with and for God; you are God's garden and vineyard and field under cultivation, [you are] God's building.

10 According to the grace (the special endowment for my task) of God bestowed on me, like a skillful architect and master builder I laid [the] foundation, and now another [man] is building upon it. But let each [man] be careful how he builds upon it,

11 For no other foundation can anyone lay than that which is [already] laid, which is Jesus Christ (the Messiah, the Anointed One).

[12] But if anyone builds upon the Foundation, whether it be with gold, silver, precious stones, wood, hay, straw,

[13] The work of each [one] will become [plainly, openly] known (shown for what it is); for the day [of Christ] will disclose and declare it, because it will be revealed with fire, and the fire will test and critically appraise the character and worth of the work each person has done.

[14] If the work which any person has built on this Foundation [any product of his efforts whatever] survives [this test], he will get his reward.

[15] But if any person's work is burned up [under the test], he will suffer the loss [of it all, losing his reward], though he himself will be saved, but only as [one who has passed] through fire." 1 Corinthians 3:9-15

Let's examine next who and what can and will block you from getting into Heaven, sending you to "the bad place."

SECTION 3

CHAPTER 12
What's Keeping You Out of Heaven

THERE ARE MANY factors that can keep a person from getting into Heaven.

We covered some hindrances to Heaven in the last Chapter that Jesus explained to us under 'Condemnations and Rewards' from The Bible book of Revelation. Jesus reveals that when assemblies/individuals of His and Bible followers accept alternatives to Him and God's Word, they didn't/won't receive their rewards. This can be through their indifference, ignorance or deliberate actions.

The lake of fire would no doubt be quite a surprising shock to these pretend followers of Jesus and the Bible.

Jesus tells us, "[13] Enter through the narrow gate; for wide is the gate and spacious and broad is the way that leads away to destruction, and many are those who are entering through it.

¹⁴ But the gate is narrow (contracted by pressure) and the way is straitened and compressed that leads away to life, and few are those who find it." Matthew 7:13-14

Examining some main dangers will assist you from being deceived, complacent or compromised by them.

Government

The world's governments consist of five main forms of power in societies being democracy, monarchy, oligarchy, authoritarianism and totalitarianism. Persecution against those who follow God's Word range from lukewarm acceptance to progressive, liberal intolerance and hostility, suppression, imprisonment, torture, and death. State controlled religion exist in countries like China, Cuba, Islamic controlled countries and Vietnam. Some countries like India persecute non-Hindus and Myanmar (Burma) oppress non-Buddhists. There are many countries where the Bible is illegal.

A follower of Jesus in Western countries such as England, Ireland, Sweden, even the USA can experience arrest for evangelizing in public (offensive language), silently praying in public (near abortion clinics) and holding private Bible studies in their home.

Government hostility against God and His true Word block billions from receiving the truth.

Educational Systems

An existing and growing trend in Western schools is a total hatred of anything God, pursuing instead indoctrination programs promoting socialism (communism, Marxism), anti-patriotism, and radical, leftist and perverse ideologies starting with 5-year-olds and into Colleges and Universities.

Anything taught about God contains their religious distortions.

Brainwashing is extensive.

Media

The media (news organizations) are voice boxes for the government. Whether right or left-leaning they are of little value other than their slant or opinions on what's truth or newsworthy.

Entertainment

Movies, music, TV, radio, video games, sports entertainers are populated by the spawn of the other systems, manipulating the planet into their versions of happiness.

Typically, all segments are antichrist.

Business

This title really encompasses all these other segments of society as they all have money-making-power-controlling agendas.

Corporations control massive amounts of global markets that influence the minds of populations. They dictate to and influence finance, governments, entertainment and the media (including internet).

God isn't factored into their equations.

Family

Families are a strong persuader in leading offspring and other members down their religious path. Families in some religions resort to ostracizing, persecution, violence and murder on their family members to achieve compliance from conversion away from their religion.

Religion

One can reasonably argue that a person's religion is the foundation of their life. Religion can be any belief system including atheism.

People's religious convictions can be formed by these other systems in this Chapter, with a mixture of their own dogma added into the mix.

Roughly 69% of the world has antibiblical ideologies. These religions, as we've discussed, rest on emotion, theories, opinions and shifting sand rather than reality.

The remaining 31% of people call themselves, Christian.

According to Wikipedia there are 47,000+ denominations and countless home groups in the world.

Close examination of these sects reveals them to be mongrels.

Mongrelite Christianity

Mongrelite-someone who is so freakishly disgusting and absolutely feral, it reminds of an actual mongrel- Urban Dictionary

Disciples (mongrelites) of mongrel religions are very prevalent in the world. They take a little bit of this and a little bit of that, with some of their own beliefs, then mix it all together to come up with their own personal mongrel religion. For many, they are the only follower of their religion on the planet.

There are numerous mongrels in the non-Christian categories and also those who mix Christianity with other ideologies thinking that they're still Christian.

The Barna Group research puts 42% of Americans in the category of being "Notional Christians," who believe in the notion or concept of Christianity in a general way but have not made a commitment to God, believing that they can earn their way into Heaven through just good moral acts.

87% of Americans polled have at least one new age belief (yougov.com). 62% of American pastors polled follow syncretism, which is an amalgamation of religions and world views (Barna Group). In other words, they're mongrels.

Highly prevalent are those who maybe hit "church" on Sunday then consult their shaman, horoscope or occultist the rest of the week.

These are just a small portion of the mongrel mentality that exist (we'll get into more later) that keep followers from getting into Heaven.

"You [are like] unfaithful wives [having illicit love affairs with the world and breaking your marriage vow to God]! Do you not know that being the world's friend is being God's enemy? So, whoever chooses to be a friend of the world takes his stand as an enemy of God." James 4:4

If you're a religious mongrel of some sort, recognize that your religion is unacceptable to God. Put it behind you. Consider it a blessing that you discovered the truth before it's too late.

Your expertise as a former religious mongrel serves others well. Guide them past these jagged rocks.

Will being a member in any of these thousands of religions get anyone into Heaven?

No.

God's Word, the Bible, His truth, is not a religion. Only you can decide that you will follow what's required to get into Heaven.

"And My eye will not spare, nor will I have pity. I will punish you according to your ways while your abominations are right in the midst of you. And you shall know, understand, and realize that it is I the Lord Who smites you." Ezekiel 7:9

Let's next examine these mongrelite Christians a little closer, who are convinced that they're on the right path into Heaven.

Maybe you're one of them.

CHAPTER 13
Mongrelite "Churches", Ministries, Seminaries, Bible Colleges and Christian Universities

Churchianity

BIBLE COLLEGES, CHRISTIAN universities, seminaries (referred to by some as "cemeteries") can be considered the root of biblical error when they produce heretical leaders. Corrupted leaders in turn produce generations of heretics through their false teachings.

"¹But also [in those days] there arose false prophets among the people, just as there will be false teachers among yourselves, who will subtly and stealthily introduce heretical doctrines (destructive heresies), even denying and disowning the Master Who bought them, bringing upon themselves swift destruction.

² And many will follow their immoral ways and lascivious doings; because of them the true Way will be maligned and defamed." 2 Peter 2:1-2

Those who claim such "educational" systems aren't that bad should examine the statistical failures of their fruit, some of which is presented in this book. Failure meaning, people suffer from failed destinies with God and worse, are doomed to the lake of fire, as they trusted leaders with their eternal lives.

A great punishment awaits such leaders.

"Not many [of you] should become teachers (self-constituted censors and reprovers of others), my brethren, for you know that we [teachers] will be judged by a higher standard and with greater severity [than other people; thus, we assume the greater accountability and the more condemnation]." James 3:1

The religious "church" conglomerate has many names and faces. For the most part, they call themselves evangelicals, fundamentalists, various orthodox, roman catholics, protestants, pentecostals, and non-denominational. They can and do add further descriptive names to themselves such as liberal, moderate, progressive, and conservative. Include yourself in if your preferred religious label has been missed.

None of these designations exist in Heaven. They're the made-up religious systems of humanity.

Amongst all of these groups, there are admittedly people who love God, but when they willingly or ignorantly embrace a mongrel religion with assortments of sinful doctrines, they expose themselves to eternal danger.

Don't be misled by others that you believe to be wise and knowledgeable, rather than researching what God says is true.

Just picking any "church" in your community, thinking they're all the same, would have the devil agree with your decision, as he doesn't care if you go to "church." He encourages religion.

Religion is a decision, whether you've given it much thought or not.

The Church is God's people, not humanity's organizational structures or buildings. The Bible's definition of Church (Greek-ecclesia) differs from what we see today. Religious "church" governments and buildings are a throw-back or holdover of the Jewish and pagan temple systems. Religion idolizes the system and buildings as holy or houses of God, rather than the person as the temple of God.

"⁴⁸ However, the Most High does not dwell in houses and temples made with hands; as the prophet says,

⁴⁹ Heaven [is] My throne, and earth the footstool for My feet. What [kind of] house can you build for Me, says the Lord, or what is the place in which I can rest?" Acts 7:48-49

"Do you not know that you are the temple of God and that the Spirit of God dwells in you?" 1 Corinthians 3:16 NKJV

Two Main Religious "Church" Systems

Typically, there are two main types of religious "church" systems. One requires strict adherence to the hierarchy's structures and doctrines; the other caters to the liberal desires of the people. Neither one hosts God first nor His Kingdom government.

What They Don't and Won't Tell You

The mongrelized, religious "church" and ministry syndicates lie to people about who they really are.

Who does God say you are?

Did you know that every living person who accepts Jesus as their only salvation to reach God and Heaven is a saint?

There are mongrel sects that have invented a process that considers only certain, qualified, and deceased individuals to be proclaimed a saint. Not only that, but these religious structures say that such dead "saints" are to be revered, prayed to, and worshipped.

You're a Saint

Saints, according to God, are those who follow God's standards. (See Psalm 31:23; Acts 9:13, 32; 26:10; Romans 8:27, 16:2; 1 Corinthians 1:2; Ephesians 4:12, 5:3; Philippians 4:21; Colossians 1:3-4, 11-13; Hebrews 6:10.) Revering, praying to, and worshipping anyone or anything but God is a dead end.

"And Jesus answered and said to him, "Get behind Me, Satan! For it is written, 'You shall worship the Lord your God, and Him only you shall serve.'" Luke 4:8

Don't accept anything else than what God says.

You're a Royal Priest

Every Christian is a royal priest of God.

"But you are a chosen race, a royal priesthood, a dedicated nation, [God's] own purchased, special people, that you may set forth the wonderful deeds and display the virtues and perfections of Him Who called you out of darkness into His marvelous light." 1 Peter 2:9

You're a Lord and King

Jesus is King of kings and Lord of lords (Revelation 19:16). Guess who these lords or rulers are? You.

The Bible says that we're seated with Jesus right now in Heaven. "Seated" meaning having power and authority as a saint, priest, and lord.

"And He raised us up together with Him and made us sit down together [giving us joint seating with Him] in the heavenly sphere [by virtue of our being] in Christ Jesus (the Messiah, the Anointed One)." Ephesians 2:6

"And if we are [His] children, then we are [His] heirs also: heirs of God and fellow heirs with Christ [sharing His inheritance with Him]; only we must share His suffering if we are to share His glory." Romans 8:17

You're a Citizen of Heaven

"But we are citizens of the state (commonwealth, homeland) which is in heaven, and from it also we earnestly and patiently await [the coming of] the Lord Jesus Christ (the Messiah) [as] Savior." Philippians 3:20

We are citizens of Heaven, His child, and a joint heir with Christ. All that Father has given Jesus is also yours.

Right now.

Religions marginalize the "laypeople" as they call them. They want them subordinate to their religious system and its leaders.

God doesn't marginalize you. He wants you to realize that you are His special child, who is a ruler in His Kingdom. Citizens, rulers and joint-heirs are always allowed into Heaven, as long as they don't give up or lose their citizenship.

But My "Church" Says...

Religious "churches", ministries and their followers are usually quite sanctimonious in how they examine those of opposing doctrines as if only their slanted version of God is acceptable to Him.

The religious wants followers to believe that God is "up there" somewhere, whom we'll see one day after we die. Until then, they expect you to attend only their "church" or ministry, sit there, listen to their approved leader, sing some songs, financially support them (heavy pressure on you to do this), and live any way you want, as long as you stay in their "church" or ministry and be under their control.

Don't accept this death trap.

Seductive Entertainment

Many "churches" and ministries have become little more than entertainment centers and social clubs, revolving around music, coffee, and food. There's nothing wrong with food and having fun as God invented it, but He wants us to seek Him and enjoy His company and get into Heaven.

"Mega-churches" and slick video productions with their "prosperity gospel" and ultra-millionaire and social media influencer "stars" have bred religious victims on a global scale, seduced under the psychological affliction known as "the lemming effect." What's truly remarkable is that many, including leaders, know God's truth yet choose to join in leading the crowd heading off the cliff.

Failing Religious Church

A 15-year study in the USA of why "so many churches are failing" by FASICLD in partnership with "Into Thy Word Ministries," revealed some startling discoveries.

*   Every year 4000 churches close their doors against 1000 new ones that start.
*   Every year 2.7 million church members fall into inactivity.
*   Half of all churches in the US do not add any new members to their ranks.
*   2-4% of Europe attends church (It's about 15% in USA).
*   Recent statistics from the Barna Group report, "that perhaps 50% of people who go to a church are not even Christian, they only go for show." In some denominations it's over 80% not Christian.

So, what are the reasons for this decay?

Excuses from "church" leaders in this study blamed "cultural decay," "changing values" and "the average American views the church with little regard." The study declared that these excuses by leaders were just symptoms of a disease. The study wanted to find out what led to these problems of cultural decay and downgrading of moral absolutes.

They asked people who left the "church" for their reasons which weren't the same reasons leaders had given. Reasons they gave for leaving are:

*   They believe the church wants their money not them
*   Ineffective teaching
*   Hypocrisy, heresy and blasphemy
*   Ineffective pastoral care

MONGRELITE "CHURCHES", MINISTRIES, SEMINARIES, BIBLE COLLEGES AND CHRISTIAN UNIVERSITIES

* Not teaching the Word or making it boring (no demonstrations of God's power, miracles, signs and wonders)
* Corrupt leaders (tolerating their own moral misdeeds and those of others)
* Was shunned, belittled, or treated with contempt or insolence
* Women say their voice doesn't matter and treated like mules
* Was manipulated and controlled
* Revolted by gossip, betrayal and backstabbing
* Turned off by conflict and strife

In the study, naïve leaders on the other hand thought failure or success depended upon such things as, "entertainment; that chairs are better than pews; storefronts are better than cathedrals; a lack of parking; power point presentations."

The study said, "The problem is the church had lost its way, we have fallen off the path that Christ has for us."

The study examined non-Christians who saw, "the "so called" evangelists who are seen on TV living lavish lifestyles... disillusioned many people." They didn't see a difference between a Christian and a non-Christian.

Avoid and Expose Mongrel Christians

Going to a "church" building or belonging to a denomination or ministry doesn't mean someone is or isn't a follower of God.

"And have no fellowship with the unfruitful works of darkness, but rather expose them" Ephesians 5: 11.

"But now I have written to you not to keep company with anyone named a brother, who is sexually immoral, or covetous, or an idolater, or a reviler, or a drunkard, or an extortioner—not even to eat with such a person" 1 Corinthians 5: 11.

God's Word says that we don't fellowship with unbelievers or sinners. Not only that, we are to warn them and expose them.

This isn't talking about evangelizing the lost, as we must walk among them to bring them to Jesus. We don't fellowship with unbelievers (infidels); deliberate sinners; heretics nor have any of them as friends nor take them in marriage.

"[12] What [business] of mine is it and what right have I to judge outsiders? Is it not those inside [the church] upon whom you are to pass disciplinary judgment [passing censuring sentence on them as the facts require]?

[13] God alone sits in judgment on those who are outside. Drive out that wicked one from among you [expel him from your church]." 1 Corinthians 5:12-13

"[14] But if anyone [in the church] refuses to obey what we say in this letter, take note of that person and do not associate with him, so that he may be ashamed.

¹⁵ Do not regard him as an enemy, but simply admonish and warn him as [being still] a brother." 2 Thessalonians 3:14-15

God's Word says that we are to judge people considered followers of God, admonish and warn them and to avoid them if they continue in their sinful ways. Don't expose yourself to the lake of fire by ignoring God's Word on this matter. Warn leaders who preach a different Gospel about their heresy. If they won't repent, then a true child of God must leave those who accept a counterfeit Gospel.

So how do we judge ourselves and others to make sure we're following God? Besides the scriptures above, there are ways that God's Word says we are to govern ourselves. A few main infections are pride, self will and fear.

Pride

Pride brought down Lucifer and brings down many leaders and non-leaders today. Avoid groups that battle each other on whose traditions and "gospel" is right. Avoid leaders who refuse to equip others for ministry or ones that manipulate others through fear, guilt, rules and restrictions, so as not to endanger their position of power and the crowd worship they desire.

Self Will

Don't be lost following your own or someone else's will (ala Lucifer), instead of God's will and His Word. Don't accommodate and compromise with sin, people and the world in some vain pursuit of fame, power, control and wealth. This can also be you or some leader making "looks good" decisions such as to start a "church" or a ministry.

Jesus <u>never</u> made "looks good" decisions nor followed His own will (John 5: 19).

God says, "And that servant who knew his master's will but did not get ready or act as he would wish him to act shall be beaten with many [lashes]." Luke 12:47 God is serious.

Fear

Those who ignore or even attack God's Truth such as the Holy Spirit power and gifts or God's truth on how to get into Heaven, are ruled by fear. They seek acceptance and credibility from the world (i.e. institutions, titles, certificates) rather than from God. They fear man (peers, family, friends) more than God. They fear losing their dignity or their paycheck. God says man's wisdom is foolishness and futile (1 Corinthians 3: 18-23).

The world's "church" is an abomination and is failing, as well as all who lead them and attend them. Attending "church" or calling oneself a Christian won't get you into Heaven.

Remember, a True child of God is the holy temple of God, not some building or piece of property.

"Do you not know that you are the temple of God and that the Spirit of God dwells in you? If anyone defiles the temple of God, God will destroy him. For the temple of God is holy, which temple you are" 1 Corinthians 3: 16-17.

Don't defile God's temple.

The Religious "Church" Is Not a Key to Heaven

Those who think or are being told that they have to "attend church" to please God or that attendance at a "church" is a key to get into Heaven are living under a false religious doctrine.

Jesus said, "For wherever two or three are gathered (drawn together as My followers) in (into) My name, there I Am in the midst of them." Matthew 18:20

I've encountered many of these types who think it's a sin to miss/not attend or be "divorced," as they call it, from "church." There's no scripture where God insists that we fellowship with the dead (spiritually). He actually tells us to avoid those, the mongrels, who aren't following His Way.

"¹⁷ I appeal to you, brethren, to be on your guard concerning those who create dissensions and difficulties and cause divisions, in opposition to the doctrine (the teaching) which you have been taught. [I warn you to turn aside from them, to] avoid them.

¹⁸ For such persons do not serve our Lord Christ but their own appetites and base desires, and by ingratiating and flattering speech, they beguile the hearts of the unsuspecting and simpleminded [people]." Romans 16:17-18

The religious "church" blocks The Way to God when they contradict Him with their personal doctrines.

"I hate, I despise your feasts, and I will not smell a savor or take delight in your solemn assemblies." Amos 5:21

Jesus said, "Uselessly do they worship Me, for they teach as doctrines the commands of men." Matthew 15:9

"¹⁶ Therefore let no one sit in judgment on you in matters of food and drink, or with regard to a feast day or a New Moon or a Sabbath.

¹⁷ Such [things] are only the shadow of things that are to come, and they have only a symbolic value. But the reality (the sub-

stance, the solid fact of what is foreshadowed, the body of it) belongs to Christ." Colossians 2:16-17

God warned us long ago… "But the [Holy] Spirit distinctly and expressly declares that in latter times some will turn away from the faith, giving attention to deluding and seducing spirits and doctrines that demons teach,." 1 Timothy 4:1

Jesus called the religious that operated in the flesh (religion) blind guides (Matthew 23:16); fools (Matthew 23:17); serpents (Matthew 23:33); generation of vipers (Matthew 23:33); hypocrites (Luke 11:44); and "Woe to you, scribes and Pharisees, pretenders (hypocrites)! For you are like tombs that have been whitewashed, which look beautiful on the outside but inside are full of dead men's bones and everything impure. Just so, you also outwardly seem to people to be just and upright but inside you are full of pretense and lawlessness and iniquity." Matthew 23:27-28

Jesus God gave us many clear warnings that we are to steer around these religious hazards.

"It is the Spirit Who gives life [He is the Life-giver]; the flesh conveys no benefit whatever [there is no profit in it]. The words (truths) that I have been speaking to you are spirit and life." John 6:63

Religious structures are death traps.

CHAPTER 14
Mongrel Leadership

Priests and Pastors are Obsolete

Religious "church" systems have organization-approved or "ordained," as they call it, leaders or ministers. Although religious leaders can be sincere and believe that they are right, mongrelization of God's Way is still harmful to them and to those who follow them. The Bible says, itchy ears like to choose leaders.

"³ For the time is coming when [people] will not tolerate (endure) sound and wholesome instruction, but, having ears itching [for something pleasing and gratifying], they will gather to themselves one teacher after another to a considerable number, chosen to satisfy their own liking and to foster the errors they hold,

⁴ And will turn aside from hearing the truth and wander off into myths and man-made fictions." 2 Timothy 4:3-4

Individual leaders, who aren't corrupted by religion, man, and the world; who are following God's will; operating fully with the Holy Spirit; and are mentors who are properly equipping the saints to do the same... God says such are worthy of honor.

"Let the elders who perform the duties of their office well be considered doubly worthy of honor [and of adequate financial support], especially those who labor faithfully in preaching and teaching." 1 Timothy 5:17

For those who do not perform well, many failures for a loss of blessings from God for people and nations can be put at the feet of such priests, pastors, and leaders. Jesus taught us to save and equip people, not produce business clients.

All over the world, denominations still have in effect the Old Testament priest system. Some lean more toward the old pagan systems. This also includes the religious "pastor system," which is just a rewording of the title "priest," operating under the same religious, old covenant hierarchy format as the ancient priest systems.

God says that the priest (and pastor) systems are obsolete. They should never have continued after Jesus' resurrection.

"In speaking of a new covenant, he makes the first one obsolete. And what is becoming obsolete and growing old is ready to vanish away." Hebrews 8:13 ESV

The brethren no longer need priests (or pastors) as Jesus is now our High Priest alone.

"[19] Therefore, brethren, since we have full freedom and confidence to enter into the [Holy of] Holies [by the power and virtue] in the blood of Jesus,

[20] By this fresh (new) and living way which He initiated and dedicated and opened for us through the separating curtain (veil of the Holy of Holies), that is, through His flesh,

[21] And since we have [such] a great and wonderful and noble Priest [Who rules] over the house of God." Hebrews 10:19-21

We now live under a better covenant.

"In keeping with [the oath's greater strength and force], Jesus has become the Guarantee of a better (stronger) agreement [a more excellent and more advantageous covenant]." Hebrews 7:22

The priest system held us captive. We operate with Jesus and the Gospel now, not under earthly priests.

"But now we are released from the law, having died to that which held us captive, so that we serve in the new way of the Spirit and not in the old way of the written code." Romans 7:6 ESV

As said in the last Chapter, every true follower of God is a royal priest of God, not some "special," religious system-appointed person (1 Peter 2:9).

Current-day priests also insist on being called "father," which is another violation of God's Word.

"And do not call anyone [in the church] on earth father, for you have one Father, Who is in heaven." Matthew 23:9

The priest systems are religious, "things of the flesh." They rob God of glory that is His alone.

"⁵For those who are according to the flesh and are controlled by its unholy desires set their minds on and pursue those things which gratify the flesh, but those who are according to the Spirit and are controlled by the desires of the Spirit set their minds on and seek those things which gratify the [Holy] Spirit.

⁶ Now the mind of the flesh [which is sense and reason without the Holy Spirit] is death [death that comprises all the miseries arising from sin, both here and hereafter]. But the mind of the [Holy] Spirit is life and [soul] peace [both now and forever].

⁷ [That is] because the mind of the flesh [with its carnal thoughts and purposes] is hostile to God, for it does not submit itself to God's Law; indeed, it cannot.

⁸ So then those who are living the life of the flesh [catering to the appetites and impulses of their carnal nature] cannot please or satisfy God, or be acceptable to Him." Romans 8:5-8

Priests and pastors are not our heads or "coverings" as they like to call it. They are not our mediators to God.

God says, "But I want you to know that the head of every man is Christ." 1 Corinthians 11:3 KJV

Pastor Dynasty

What does God say that we are to do with those who oppose His Gospel?

"[As for] a man who is factious [a heretical sectarian and cause of divisions], after admonishing him a first and second time, reject [him from your fellowship and have nothing more to do with him]." Titus 3:10 also Romans 16:17-18

Entire religious structures revolve around "pastors" being mentioned just once in the New Testament (Ephesians 4:11), after apostles, prophets, and evangelists. The mature in Christ's function is to equip and serve the spiritual babies in Christ, to help them grow and mature into spiritual adults; into their intimate relationship and destinies with God; to show them The Way to God and into Heaven; not to lord themselves over them.

"²⁵ And Jesus called them to Him and said, You know that the rulers of the Gentiles lord it over them, and their great men hold them in subjection [tyrannizing over them].

²⁶ Not so shall it be among you; but whoever wishes to be great among you must be your servant,

²⁷ And whoever desires to be first among you must be your slave—

²⁸ Just as the Son of Man came not to be waited on but to serve, and to give His life as a ransom for many [the price paid to set them free].' " Matthew 20:25-28

Anything else is a false leader.

Those Cursed by God

God says anyone who speaks or follows a false gospel are cursed.

"⁶I am surprised and astonished that you are so quickly turning renegade and deserting Him Who invited and called you by the grace (unmerited favor) of Christ (the Messiah) [and that you are transferring your allegiance] to a different [even an opposition] gospel.

⁷ Not that there is [or could be] any other [genuine Gospel], but there are [obviously] some who are troubling and disturbing and

bewildering you [with a different kind of teaching which they offer as a gospel] and want to pervert and distort the Gospel of Christ (the Messiah) [into something which it absolutely is not].

⁸ But even if we or an angel from heaven should preach to you a gospel contrary to and different from that which we preached to you, let him be accursed (anathema, devoted to destruction, doomed to eternal punishment)!

⁹ As we said before, so I now say again: If anyone is preaching to you a gospel different from or contrary to that which you received [from us], let him be accursed (anathema, devoted to destruction, doomed to eternal punishment)!

¹⁰ Now am I trying to win the favor of men, or of God? Do I seek to please men? If I were still seeking popularity with men, I should not be a bond servant of Christ (the Messiah)." Galatians 1:6-10

The priest/pastor-religious systems that are in operation in the world today are in direct contradiction to God's Word.

"But woe to you, scribes and Pharisees, pretenders (hypocrites)! For you shut the kingdom of heaven in men's faces; for you neither enter yourselves, nor do you allow those who are about to go in to do so." Matthew 23:13

Don't be cursed by God or follow those who are cursed. As God says, avoid them. If you are one, repent and get right with God. More on repentance later.

Wolves

God also warns us of a particular nasty breed that can destroy us. They can hide under shepherd's cloaks or the sheepskins of the flock.

Wolves lead people away from God and Heaven.

Jesus warns us, "Beware of false prophets, who come to you dressed as sheep, but inside they are devouring wolves." Matthew 7:15

"[29] I know that after I am gone, ferocious wolves will get in among you, not sparing the flock;

[30] Even from among your own selves men will come to the front who, by saying perverse (distorted and corrupt) things, will endeavor to draw away the disciples after them [to their own party]." Acts 20:29-30

Jude warns us of them, as does all of 2 Peter 2, who details their destructive doctrines; the doom of false teachers; the depravity of false teachers; the deceptions of false teachers.

In brief, these false prophets and false teachers have lost their salvation, and their judgment is assured, as well as those who follow their lies (2 Corinthians 11:12-15).

Predatory Evil Leaders

Examine what leaders and those you associate with are saying and doing. Don't base your decision on their charisma or how many aircraft they own. Examine it all closely as it is your life that will be affected now and when you stand in front of God one day at your judgment. Each person is accountable for their own actions.

Beware of the wolves when you need mentors to be equipped for God, and when fellowshipping with others.

Jesus said, "[8] These people draw near Me with their mouths and honor Me with their lips, but their hearts hold off and are far away from Me.

[9] Uselessly do they worship Me, for they teach as doctrines the commands of men." Matthew 15:8-9

He also said, "Let them alone and disregard them; they are blind guides and teachers. And if a blind man leads a blind man, both will fall into a ditch." Matthew 15:14

God says avoid <u>false and deceptive</u> leaders, as well as those who <u>pretend</u> to be followers of God to deliberately destroy others as well as those who <u>think</u> they're saved. You have nothing in common with enemies of God, non-believers, deliberate sinners and compromisers of His Word.

Any and all wolves are dangerous and deadly.

Jesus openly confronted these predators in His ministry:

"But when he saw many of the Pharisees and Sadducees coming for baptism, he said to them, You brood of vipers! Who warned you to flee and escape from the wrath and indignation [of God against disobedience] that is coming?" Matthew 3:7/Luke 3:7

"You offspring of vipers! How can you speak good things when you are evil (wicked)? For out of the fullness (the overflow, the superabundance) of the heart the mouth speaks." Matthew 12:34

"You serpents! You spawn of vipers! How can you escape the penalty to be suffered in hell (Gehenna)?" Matthew 23:33

And He warned us of the wolves, "Behold, I am sending you out like sheep in the midst of wolves; be wary and wise as serpents, and be innocent (harmless, guileless, and without falsity) as doves." Matthew 10:16/Luke 10:3

Notice that Jesus openly confronts these false leaders, rather than just ignoring them and their activities.

Besides Jesus warning us of these enemies in the camp, we can see that Jude felt it necessary to warn us also:

"Beloved, my whole concern was to write to you in regard to our common salvation. [But] I found it necessary and was impelled to write you and urgently appeal to and exhort [you] to contend for the faith which was once for all handed down to the saints [the faith which is that sum of Christian belief which was delivered verbally to the holy people of God]." Jude 3

Jude wanted to write about salvation, yet was led by God instead to urge or insist that we fight against a certain foe, for the faith which was given to us.

He next tells us who is attacking the followers of God, "For certain men have crept in stealthily [gaining entrance secretly by a side door]. Their doom was predicted long ago, ungodly (impious, profane) persons who pervert the grace (the spiritual blessing and favor) of our God into lawlessness and wantonness and immorality, and disown and deny our sole Master and Lord, Jesus Christ (the Messiah, the Anointed One)." Jude 4

Sons and Daughters of Belial

They deliberately hide their true intentions. They are not deceived, they are ungodly. They covertly operate to destroy and deceive... they are also called the sons and daughters of Belial by God.

There are those (wolves) who try to lead others to false gods, false religions, and false doctrines:

"Certain men, <u>the children of Belial</u>, are gone out from among you, and have withdrawn the inhabitants of their city, saying, Let us go and serve other gods, which ye have not known." Deuteronomy 13:13 KJV

They can be unholy ministry leaders who steal, commit adultery, purposely sin, refuse to serve the Lord, refuse to repent, even if found out.

"Now the sons of Eli (priests) were <u>sons of Belial</u>; they knew not the LORD." 1 Samuel 2:12 KJV

And they can also be women: "Count not thine handmaid for a <u>daughter of Belial</u>: for out of the abundance of my complaint and grief have I spoken hitherto." 1 Samuel 1:16 KJV

Quoting from <u>Goetia</u>, "Belial is the demon of lies and guilt. As a Prince of Hell, he commands 80 Legions of Demons and is specifically the prince reigning over the Northern Reaches of

Hell. It controls the elements of earth and reigns over the Earth Elementals (earth demons)."

Many also consider Belial to be just another in a long stream of names for satan.

There is a difference between this kind, and those who are just deceived. The sons and daughters of Belial have intentionally decided to be wicked to destroy others.

The Bible calls them wicked, lewd, worthless, vipers, wolves, murderers, lustful, liars, deceivers, and the seed or children of the devil.

Don't have any of these in your life.

Jude gives us some similarities to compare them with:

"Woe unto them! for they have gone in the way of Cain, and ran greedily after the error of Balaam for reward, and perished in the gainsaying of Core." Jude 11 KJV

Jude mentions Cain, Balaam and Core in this verse. Cain was a murderer (Genesis 4); Balaam was a prophet who sold out Israel (Numbers 22-25); Core or Korah, was a Levite (minister) who was a rebel, leading others to himself (Numbers 16). All of them were enemies of God.

Jude warns us that these kinds are amongst us and in our gatherings, intending to destroy and deceive:

"These are spots in your feasts of charity, when they feast with you, feeding themselves without fear." Jude 12a

So how do we know one of these particular "flesh and blood" infiltrators, who are hiding in the midst of us and set on destroying us?

AND, how do <u>we</u> combat them?

Many are pretty obvious and easy to spot as they are "murmurers, complainers, walking after their own lusts." Jude 16 and Jude 19, "sensual, having not the spirit."

Some are not so easy to spot.

How to Test Leaders

These wolves can act in various ways, yet they can be spotted by their "fruit" which is usually non-existent.

"These are spots in your feasts of charity, when they feast with you, feeding themselves without fear." 1 John 4:1

"[16] By their fruit you will recognize them. Do people pick grapes from thornbushes, or figs from thistles?

¹⁷ Likewise, every good tree bears good fruit, but a bad tree bears bad fruit.

¹⁸ A good tree cannot bear bad fruit, and a bad tree cannot bear good fruit.

¹⁹ Every tree that does not bear good fruit is cut down and thrown into the fire.

²⁰ Thus, by their fruit you will recognize them." Matthew 7:16-20 NIV

When God says fruit He means what He considers fruit, not what people consider fruit.

Corrupt Leader Fruit

What does God consider bad fruit from a leader or shepherd of the flock?

In Ezekiel 34 God commands Ezekiel to speak out against bad shepherds with a list of 14 sins:

1. Feed themselves without feeding the flock (v. 2)
2. Eat the fat and clothe themselves with wool, but don't feed the flock. (v. 3)
3. Kill them that are fed (v. 3)
4. Have not strengthened the diseased. (v. 4)

5. Have not healed the sick (v. 4)
6. Have not bound up the broken (v. 4)
7. Have not brought again that which was driven away. (v. 4)
8. Have not sought the lost. (v. 4, 6)
9. Oppressed their subjects. (v. 4)
10. Scattered the flock. (v. 5)
11. Have not been true shepherds (v. 5)
12. Caused flock to be destroyed. (v. 5)
13. Have not protected the flock (v. 5)
14. Ignored the true condition of the flock (v. 6)

These wolves are in "churches" and ministries all over the world today.

Some wolves are more interested in wages, conference fees, partner fees, tithes and offerings and their power lifestyle, than caring for sheep. A true shepherd goes to God for their needs, not the world.

Some wolves don't strengthen or heal sheep to prepare them to reproduce more sheep (evangelize). A true shepherd teaches and promotes God's children to produce good fruit (i.e. follow His perfect will).

Some wolves drive away sheep with their force, pride, cruelty, control and manipulation. Their will is supreme. They won't admit errors and expect others to overlook their errors. They demand loyalty. They won't try to protect sheep, find them nor bring them back. A true shepherd will lovingly guide and protect the flock and hunt for any that go missing to find out why, fix what is wrong and try to bring them back.

Some wolves prefer to be entertainers and business-minded, not interested in correcting, rebuking, nor expelling those that refuse to repent. A true shepherd teaches the flock the entire Word of God and what is expected of them to obtain God's blessings and salvation. A true shepherd will expel all those rebellious and disobedient to God from the flock, to preserve the faithful sheep.

Remove Wolves

All wolves that have left the sheep to be prey (v. 8) need to voluntarily remove themselves from the flock to save themselves from God's 8-fold judgment:

1. Woe to them. (v. 2)
2. I am against them. (v. 10)
3. I will require My flock of them. (v. 10)
4. Their dominion will be taken away (v. 10)
5. They will not feed themselves again. (v. 10)
6. I will deliver my flock from them. (v. 10)
7. I will destroy them. (v. 16)
8. I will feed them with judgment. (v. 16)

Wolves who refuse to leave voluntarily (usually the case as wolves won't admit they're a wolf), need to be expelled by the sheep.

Covering this again, after teaching the Gospel to the Ephesians for 3 years, Paul left them with perhaps his most important message...

"²⁸ Therefore, take heed to yourselves and to all the flock, among which the Holy Spirit has made you overseers, to shepherd the church of God which He purchased with His own blood.

²⁹ <u>For I know this</u>, that after my departure <u>savage wolves will come in among you, not sparing the flock</u>.

³⁰ Also from among yourselves men will rise up, speaking perverse things, to draw away the disciples after themselves.

³¹ Therefore watch, and remember that for three years I did not cease to warn everyone night and day with tears." Acts 20:28-31 NKJV

The Ephesians didn't listen to Paul's warning as false teaching became a major problem there.

Paul later asked Timothy to help them... "³ As I urged you when I went into Macedonia—remain in Ephesus that you may charge some that they teach no other doctrine,

"⁴ Nor give heed to fables and endless genealogies, which cause disputes rather than godly edification which is in faith." 1 Timothy 1:3-4 NKJV

Jesus warned the Ephesians through John in Revelation 2:4-5, 30 years after Paul and Timothy warned them.

The Ephesians were obviously holding congregational meetings, worship services, teaching and praying in the name of Jesus, and <u>considered themselves to be followers of God</u>, but they were following false leaders and false doctrine as truth. People trusted and believed what these false leaders said to them.

The "ravenous wolves" in Ephesus were separating the one true Shepherd Jesus from His flock, with deception and false teaching; leading them to their doom.

2 Peter 2 is Peter's warning that further defines this enemy and God's position with them.

Destructive Doctrines

"¹ But also [in those days] there arose false prophets among the people, just as there will be false teachers among yourselves, who will subtly and stealthily introduce heretical doctrines (destructive heresies), even denying and disowning the Master Who bought them, bringing upon themselves swift destruction.

² And many will follow their immoral ways and lascivious doings; because of them the true Way will be maligned and defamed.

³ And in their covetousness (lust, greed) they will exploit you with false (cunning) arguments. From of old the sentence [of condemnation] for them has not been idle; their destruction (eternal misery) has not been asleep.

Doom of False Teachers

⁴ For God did not [even] spare angels that sinned, but cast them into hell, delivering them to be kept there in pits of gloom till the judgment and their doom.

⁵ And He spared not the ancient world, but preserved Noah, a preacher of righteousness, with seven other persons, when He brought a flood upon the world of ungodly [people].

⁶ And He condemned to ruin and extinction the cities of Sodom and Gomorrah, reducing them to ashes [and thus] set them forth as an example to those who would be ungodly;

⁷ And He rescued righteous Lot, greatly worn out and distressed by the wanton ways of the ungodly and lawless—

⁸ For that just man, living [there] among them, tortured his righteous soul every day with what he saw and heard of [their] unlawful and wicked deeds—

⁹ Now if [all these things are true, then be sure] the Lord knows how to rescue the godly out of temptations and trials, and how to keep the ungodly under chastisement until the day of judgment and doom,

¹⁰ And particularly those who walk after the flesh and indulge in the lust of polluting passion and scorn and despise authority. Presumptuous [and] daring [self-willed and self-loving creatures]! They scoff at and revile dignitaries (glorious ones) without trembling,

¹¹ Whereas [even] angels, though superior in might and power, do not bring a defaming charge against them before the Lord.

Depravity of False Teachers

¹² But these [people]! Like unreasoning beasts, mere creatures of instinct, born [only] to be captured and destroyed, railing at things of which they are ignorant, they shall utterly perish in their [own] corruption [in their destroying they shall surely be destroyed],

¹³ Being destined to receive [punishment as] the reward of [their] unrighteousness [suffering wrong as the hire for their wrongdoing]. They count it a delight to revel in the daytime [living luxuriously and delicately]. They are blots and blemishes, reveling in their deceptions and carousing together [even] as they feast with you.

¹⁴ They have eyes full of harlotry, insatiable for sin. They beguile and bait and lure away unstable souls. Their hearts are trained in covetousness (lust, greed), [they are] children of a curse [exposed to cursing]!

¹⁵ Forsaking the straight road they have gone astray; they have followed the way of Balaam [the son] of Beor, who loved the reward of wickedness.

¹⁶ But he was rebuked for his own transgression when a dumb beast of burden spoke with human voice and checked the prophet's madness.

¹⁷ These are springs without water and mists driven along before a tempest, for whom is reserved forever the gloom of darkness.

Deceptions of False Teachers

¹⁸ For uttering loud boasts of folly, they beguile and lure with lustful desires of the flesh those who are barely escaping from them who are wrongdoers.

¹⁹ They promise them liberty, when they themselves are the slaves of depravity and defilement—for by whatever anyone is made inferior or worse or is overcome, to that [person or thing] he is enslaved.

²⁰ For if, after they have escaped the pollutions of the world through [the full, personal] knowledge of our Lord and Savior

Jesus Christ, they again become entangled in them and are overcome, their last condition is worse [for them] than the first.

[21] For never to have obtained a [full, personal] knowledge of the way of righteousness would have been better for them than, having obtained [such knowledge], to turn back from the holy commandment which was [verbally] delivered to them.

[22] There has befallen them the thing spoken of in the true proverb, The dog turns back to his own vomit, and, the sow is washed only to wallow again in the mire."

Tools of satan

Many wolves deceive themselves and/or are deceived into thinking that they're good shepherds, but they are still a tool of satan.

They may look good, seem sincere and sound good, but examine the fruit to see if they're wolf or shepherd.

Does their teaching hold up to God's Word?

Do they fall into <u>any</u> of the categories listed in Ezekiel 34?

Do they live in, practice, accept or compromise with sin (sexual immorality, lying, stealing, gossip, idolatry, drunkenness, etc.)?

Are they producing, encouraging and equipping sheep?

Do they bring God's standards to the world or the world's standards to the people?

Do the sheep they're responsible for, know God's truth?

Statistics on Mongrel Christians

Let's examine some examples of what false leaders and wolves have produced in America, which can be considered worse in some regions like Europe.

A major US nationwide survey of adults spiritual beliefs by The Barna Group in April 2009 says that Americans who <u>consider</u> themselves to be Christian have a diverse set of beliefs – but many of those beliefs are contradictory or, at least, inconsistent.

* 59% of Christians said they believed that satan "is not a living being but is just a <u>symbol</u> of evil." (Only 26% of Christians surveyed believed satan is a real entity)

* 38% believe the Holy Spirit is just a <u>symbol</u> of God's power… He's not a living being. Another 20% agreed somewhat that the Holy Spirit is just a symbol (58% haven't a clue Who the Holy Spirit is)

* Only 55% of Christians believe the Bible is accurate

* 33% of Christians believe the Bible, Quran and Book of Mormon teach the same truths

Of the 12 largest denominations studied, "only 41% <u>could be classified as "born again"</u>.

Barna Group's survey didn't allow for additional factors, which is why they probably said "could be classified as born-again."

A 2023 Arizonia Christian University study revealed a decline from the Barna Group survey:

* 1% of preteens have a Biblical worldview

* 21% of born-again teens believe they will live with God in eternity because of a personal decision to trust Christ, <u>but nearly double that believe in reincarnation</u>

* 61% either accept that Jesus sinned while he was on earth or believe it's possible

* 62% of Americans holds at least one New Age belief

There are people who think they're Christian because their parents were.

There are people who think they're Christian because they went to church when they were a child.

There are people who think they're Christian because they accepted Jesus, years ago, but continued their sinful lifestyle.

There are people who think they're a Christian because they own a Bible and wear a cross around their neck.

Convincing someone who thinks they're a follower of God that they're really a lost mongrel is close to a fool's errand.

"Religious" seminaries/training centers, denominational/ministry "businesses" and false leaders, who are people pleasers, accepters and compromisers of sin, teachers of false doctrines, are to blame for these abysmal statistics and testimonies.

These statistics don't include all the billions of people in the world that never became nor considered themselves followers of God, due to the failure of these wolves to fulfill the "Great Commission" (discussed later) and their sub-standard spiritual lifestyles that people aren't drawn to.

Some other teeth on the wolf include their promoting or accepting backstabbing, slander and gossip. Satan's goal here is to destroy you with your own words.

"[36] But I tell you, on the day of judgment men will have to give account for every idle (inoperative, nonworking) word they speak.

⁣³⁷ For by your words you will be justified and acquitted, and by your words you will be condemned and sentenced." Matthew 12:36-37

Mongrelized Salvation

Wolves also teach salvation is possible with other than Jesus Christ, such as through works or being a "good" person or the "once saved, always saved" false doctrine. They've come up with their own salvation rules that they accept or that others want to hear.

Beware of those proclaiming themselves to be apostles, prophets, generals and who knows what else, when they act like wolves.

Paul warns of this kind, "¹² But what I do, I will continue to do, [for I am determined to maintain this independence] in order to cut off the claim of those who would like [to find an occasion and incentive] to claim that in their boasted [mission] they work on the same terms that we do.

¹³ For such men are false apostles [spurious, counterfeits], deceitful workmen, masquerading as apostles (special messengers) of Christ (the Messiah).

¹⁴ And it is no wonder, for Satan himself masquerades as an angel of light;

[15] So it is not surprising if his servants also masquerade as ministers of righteousness. [But] their end will correspond with their deeds." 2 Corinthians 11:12-15

Some have such a prideful, jealous and controlling spirit that they will even override the Holy Spirit's directions given to others, thinking that only they know what is best, and that only they hear from God.

Such wolves can be quite vile and ruthless. They suffer from a dysfunctional syndrome typical of dictators, the mafia, cult leaders or territorial spirits.

This kind can appear loving, helpful and friendly, but when they feel any challenge to the lofty position, they imagine they possess, be ready for an attack.

They usually command and expect total loyalty and surrender to their will. Many insist that they be "your covering" before you will be allowed to do anything with them or in "their" ministry.

Paul teaches… "For when one says, "I am of Paul," and another, "I am of Apollos," are you not carnal?" I Corinthians 3:4

In other words, you don't belong to a person.

"For we are fellow workmen (joint promoters, laborers together) with and for God; you are God's Garden and vineyard and field under cultivation, [you are] God's building." 1 Corinthians 3:9

In other words, God is our covering, not man.

"¹⁴ For all who are led by the Spirit of God are sons of God.

¹⁵ For [the Spirit which] you have now received [is] not a spirit of slavery to put you once more in bondage to fear, but you have received the Spirit of adoption [the Spirit producing sonship] in [the bliss of] which we cry, Abba (Father)! Father!

¹⁶ The Spirit Himself [thus] testifies together with our own spirit, [assuring us] that we are children of God.

¹⁷ And if we are [His] children, then we are [His] heirs also: heirs of God and fellow heirs with Christ [sharing His inheritance with Him]; only we must share His suffering if we are to share His glory." Romans 8:14-17

Father and Jesus paid a heavy price for this blessing for us. Anyone who presumes to take control of this blessing from us is a liar and a thief… a wolf. Don't let them get away with it for you or anyone else.

Jesus is your only Mediator

No other mediator but Jesus is needed to go directly to Father.

New followers of God need direction, guidance and nurturing... they don't need a human master... they need a humble servant... a guide.

"¹ I warn and counsel the elders among you (the pastors and spiritual guides of the church) as a fellow elder and as an eyewitness [called to testify] of the sufferings of Christ, as well as a sharer in the glory (the honor and splendor) that is to be revealed (disclosed, unfolded):

² Tend (nurture, guard, guide, and fold) the flock of God that is [your responsibility], not by coercion or constraint, but willingly; not dishonorably motivated by the advantages and profits [belonging to the office], but eagerly and cheerfully;

³ Not domineering [as arrogant, dictatorial, and overbearing persons] over those in your charge, but being examples (patterns and models of Christian living) to the flock (the congregation).

⁴ And [then] when the Chief Shepherd is revealed, you will win the conqueror's crown of glory." 1 Peter 5:1-4

Wolves who command obedience and "lord" over people are not pleased with those they think are intruders or competition… they view them as a threat to their position.

I've been attacked behind my back by very unlikely sources so keep checking your back with the Holy Spirit for a "head's up" of any wolves in league against you, even if they are a distance away.

Corrupt leaders in the Bible were exposed by those who operated in the spirit such as Moses, David, Elijah, Peter, Paul, Jude, and Jesus.

<u>They were exposed, not ignored.</u>

By operating in the spirit, they knew who the wolves were.

God exposes them the same way today.

If a person is not operating with the Holy Spirit, they are operating blind.

Jude 20-23 tells us how to <u>prepare and defend</u> ourselves 7 ways from these "brute beasts" (v. 10):

1. But you, beloved, building up yourselves on your most holy faith,
2. Praying in the Holy Spirit,
3. Keep yourselves in the love of God,

4. Looking for the mercy of our Lord Jesus Christ unto eternal life
5. And of some have compassion, making a difference
6. And others save with fear, pulling them out of the fire;
7. Hating even the garment spotted by the flesh

Jude 24 tells us that God can do two things:

1. Now unto him that is able to keep you from falling,
2. And to present you faultless before the presence of his glory with exceeding joy.

Repent Wolves or Face God's Wrath

If you are a leader now, check yourself for your faults against what God expects of you in His Word. If you have failed the test, repent as David did and be restored to God and properly direct the flock <u>or face destruction</u>.

"But woe to you, scribes and Pharisees, pretenders (hypocrites)! For you shut the kingdom of heaven in men's faces; for you neither enter yourselves, nor do you allow those who are about to go in to do so." Matthew 23:13

Notice in the scripture above, false leadership and false teachings shuts off the sheep from Heaven.

It is every person's responsibility to insure they are right with God. When standing at judgment in front of God one day, you

<u>can</u> blame your life on the wolves, but that won't be an acceptable defense.

Many leaders start out as shepherds and because of greed, sin, pride, self-glory, indifference, etc., they become a wolf.

For any who are led to be leaders, be careful that you don't become a wolf of satan… "My brethren, let not many of you become teachers, knowing that <u>we shall receive a stricter judgment</u>. For we all stumble in many things." James 3:1-2 NJKV

Oddly… sheep ("pretend sheep") have a greater tendency to remove a true shepherd from their midst; preferring a wolf that appeases them.

These pretend sheep and head wolves will get their day in court.

Remember… the enemy isn't always out in front of you and doesn't always look like a wolf.

Replacing wolves and mongrel leaders with true shepherds of God would destroy the religious and ideological strongholds that are blocking people from getting into Heaven.

It can start with you. Be an influencer.

Recommended reading... Frank Viloa and George Barna, *Pagan Christianity*, Tyndale House, Revised and Updated Edition 2012

This volume reveals the startling truth: most of what Christians do in present-day "churches" is not rooted in the New Testament, but in pagan culture and rituals developed long after the death of the apostles. Coauthors Frank Viola and George Barna support their thesis with compelling historical evidence to document the full story of modern Christian church practices.

CHAPTER 15
Mongrel Congregation, Laypeople, the Flock, Parishioners

THE MONGRELIZATION OF the world's Christianity is statistically proven to be over 95%.

There are doctrines and beliefs that range from the fantastically silly to the satanically obvious.

Religion has many facets that need to be thoroughly examined so you can be aware of its death traps.

Religious "churches" and ministries made up of leaders and followers, have invented doctrines over the centuries to fit their religious ideologies. Adherents become very outraged when you question their path when compared to what God says in the Bible.

The Religious Zealots

We discussed in the last chapter that leaders and non-leaders can be deceived, corrupt and even wolves.

Perhaps the most challenging to reach with God's truth can be those who think that their manufactured doctrines are absolute. The zealots.

"Therefore, let anyone who thinks he stands [who feels sure that he has a steadfast mind and is standing firm], take heed lest he fall [into sin]." 1 Corinthains 10:12

A caustic statement issued by various zealot denominations is, "Only our church and its members are the true church because... (fill in the blank)." In other words, it's like they're saying, "only *we* are going to Heaven." Yes, there are those who actually make that statement.

Such proclamations are absurd and a sin.

As mentioned in the last Chapter, Jesus spoke to religious Pharisees, "But I tell you, on the day of judgment men will have to give account for every idle (inoperative, nonworking) word they speak. For by your words, you will be justified and acquitted, and by your words you will be condemned and sentenced." Matthew 12:36-37

Religious zealots are not our standard; God is.

There are no "magic church tickets." Masquerading as a Christian doesn't work with God any more than it did for the Pharisees.

Jesus said, "Not everyone who says to Me, 'Not everyone who says to Me, Lord, Lord, will enter the kingdom of heaven, but he who does the will of My Father Who is in heaven. Many will say to Me on that day, Lord, Lord, have we not prophesied in Your name and driven out demons in Your name and done many mighty works in Your name? And then I will say to them openly (publicly), I never knew you; depart from Me, you who act wickedly [disregarding My commands].'" Matthew 7:21-23

Even with proof of what God wants and expects of them, zealots will usually cling to their religion. Just look to all the Pharisees and Sadducees who saw and heard of miracles, signs and wonders from Jesus for over three years, yet, refused to abandon their legalism, their religion, their lofty positions, and their pride to embrace Jesus. The same religious mongrels exist today.

Zealots even make the Bible their god not accepting anything that isn't mentioned in the Bible. God says, "[It is He] Who has qualified us [making us to be fit and worthy and sufficient] as ministers and dispensers of a new covenant [of salvation through Christ], not [ministers] of the letter (of legally written code) but of the Spirit; for the code [of the Law] kills, but the [Holy] Spirit makes alive." 2 Corinthians 3:6.

Oddly, if they truly followed their own religious principles, by adhering to only what it says in the Bible, miracles, signs and wonders should take place after every Gospel sermon, as Jesus taught, and the Bible directs us to do (1 Corinthians 2:1-5; Acts 14:1-3; Romans 15:19). The Bible doesn't contain God, it points to Him.

Legalists reject anything outside of the precedent of the Bible. "If it didn't happen in the Bible," they say, "then it can't be God." They fear the possibility that they may be deceived, so they dismiss everything else. God doesn't confine Himself in a box. By dismissing everything, they fall into the devil's plan for them, to reject what God has for their lives.

The religious zealot criticizes those who follow God's supernatural Way. Christians who have been taught against the supernatural and manifestations of spiritual gifts wallow in their religion. They don't believe in supernatural occurrences. Unbelief is a safe position for them. They get what they pursue... nothing. They religiously embrace the mediocre as they are lazy and in fear of change. They resist change, preferring to make themselves look pure and Godly with their rituals. Those who have God power threaten and frighten those who don't.

Wallowing in religion or with the religious doesn't provide true or lasting love, peace, joy, blessings or fulfillment nor will it get you into Heaven.

Mad at God

People are mad at God for various reasons such as they blame God for all their problems and the evil condition of the world and so, either refuse to believe God exists or angrily refuse to acknowledge Him or follow His ways.

God gave the world to humans to look after. Humans run it into the ground when they choose to run it outside of God's standards.

"The heavens are the Lord's heavens, but the earth has He given to the children of men." Psalm 115:16

God gave each person free will to choose His path or their own path in life.

"All things are legitimate [permissible—and we are free to do anything we please], but not all things are helpful (expedient, profitable, and wholesome). All things are legitimate, but not all things are constructive [to character] and edifying [to spiritual life]." 1 Corinthians 10:23

It would profit a person more to be mad at the devil, than God.

"Be well balanced (temperate, sober of mind), be vigilant and cautious at all times; for that enemy of yours, the devil, roams around like a lion roaring [in fierce hunger], seeking someone to seize upon and devour." 1 Peter 5:8

People get turned off from God because of the way mongrelized Christians act or how they were treated by them. I understand the antagonism people have against fake Christians for their heresy, blasphemy, hypocrisy, holier-than-thou attitudes, back-stabbing, money-grabbing, prideful, power tripping ways, as I've seen and experienced all of it, but don't confuse God with religious systems and their acolytes.

Jesus said we should expect to be hated, rejected and betrayed, "And you will be hated by all for My name's sake, but he who perseveres and endures to the end will be saved [from spiritual disease and death in the world to come]." Matthew 10:22

He also said, "[18] If the world hates you, know that it hated Me before it hated you.

[19] If you belonged to the world, the world would treat you with affection and would love you as its own. But because you are not of the world [no longer one with it], but I have chosen (selected) you out of the world, the world hates (detests) you.

[20] Remember that I told you, A servant is not greater than his master [is not superior to him]. If they persecuted Me, they

will also persecute you; if they kept My word and obeyed My teachings, they will also keep and obey yours.

[21] But they will do all this to you [inflict all this suffering on you] because of [your bearing] My name and on My account, for they do not know or understand the One Who sent Me." John 15:18-21

Even if you end up alone because you refuse to follow delusional, mongrelized doctrines, don't despair or yield under any pressure. Keep your eyes on Heaven. You have plenty of family there.

Jesus said, "For whoever does the things God wills is My brother and sister and mother!" Mark 3:35

CHAPTER 16
Religion Worse than Sin

"²¹ FOR NEVER TO have obtained a [full, personal] knowledge of the way of righteousness would have been better for them than, having obtained [such knowledge], to turn back from the holy commandment which was [verbally] delivered to them.

²² There has befallen them the thing spoken of in the true proverb, The dog turns back to his own vomit, and, The sow is washed only to wallow again in the mire." 2 Peter 2:21-22 NKJV

Many people don't see the harm in attending a religious "church," as they'll say that they're "nice" people there who do "good." There's nothing wrong with these characteristics, but God's Word outlines what He expects from us, especially leaders, to fulfill His will. Many believe that they can mostly do what God says but can also live in gray (counterfeit) areas too.

God says that isn't acceptable.

The Poison Pills

"Your glorying is not good. Do you not know that a little leaven leavens the whole lump? Therefore, purge out the old leaven, that you may be a new lump, since you truly are unleavened." 1 Corinthians 5:6-7 NKJV

I've listened to countless leaders and people, even international known ones, saying all the right things except for one or a few false doctrines that they profess. For instance, I've heard one teach that the dead can be prayed out of hell or can be released from hell.

Universalists believe God's grace and love will eventually bring everyone into Heaven including satan. This false doctrine is saying that what Jesus did for us is a lie and what God clearly states in the Bible on entering Heaven is a lie.

These antichrist doctrines are poison pills.

Don't swallow poison no matter who offers it to you.

The Bible tells us how terrible religion is in Matthew 11:20-24 when Jesus warned that the religious people in Chorazin, Bethsaida, and Capernaum would be judged more harshly than those in the sin cities of Tyre, Sidon, and Sodom. He was saying that even in these cities of sin, had they witnessed the miracles of Jesus, they would have left sin to go embrace Him. The religious in Chorazin, Bethsaida, and Capernaum chose religion over Jesus. Religion is even more terrible than sin.

This statement, of course, would shock most Christians. Many enjoy their religious ways, even when there are the miracles and wonders of God, but few genuinely abandon their religion to make Him their focus in life.

For many who have left the religious "church," such news is a welcome relief and justification of their actions, as many have been labelled "rebels" and "lone rangers" and sinners. The Bible is full of "lone rangers" who walked with God, while others preferred floundering in the world and their religions.

Heavenly Choices

As God has pointed out in the Bible, religion is a deadly choice for those who seek a home in Heaven.

God's Way is not open for debate, opinion, massaging, contradiction, compromise or watering down in order to appease our sensibilities or for political correctness. We're not His boss. Man's ways are foolish.

"[18] Let no person deceive himself. If anyone among you supposes that he is wise in this age, let him become a fool [let him discard his worldly discernment and recognize himself as dull, stupid, and foolish, without true learning and scholarship], that he may become [really] wise.

[19] For this world's wisdom is foolishness (absurdity and stupidity) with God, for it is written, He lays hold of the wise in their [own] craftiness;

[20] And again, The Lord knows the thoughts and reasonings of the [humanly] wise and recognizes how futile they are.' " 1 Corinthians 3:18-20

Examine Yourself

Each of us must examine ourselves to see where we are in our position with God. Are we a self-pleaser, a man-pleaser, a world-pleaser, a religion-pleaser or a God-pleaser?

Many people today, turned off by the religious "church," start home groups to get away from religion. Some call them "organic churches." Yet, many become just another religious group operating under flesh-designed, self-willed programs/leaders. If you start or attend one of them, beware, as religion also creeps into groups that can start out under God.

You have to get past the "dog and pony shows." When people call you a rebel because you're doing something that isn't under their "covering" or "accepted doctrine," remind them that the religious "experts" of Jesus' day called Him a rebellious heretic.

Many of those of God in the Bible carried the same label from the religious establishment.

It's no wonder people run away from "churches" when they're full of heretics and hypocrites.

"If I am not doing the works [performing the deeds] of My Father, then do not believe Me [do not adhere to Me and trust Me and rely on Me]." John 10:37

The religious may call you a fake or deceived or "of the devil" when you compare what they're doing to the Bible. They don't want to admit they're wrong to abandon their belief system, their family, their friends and for some their power and paycheck. It's easier to attack you. Any time they attack you, keep in mind that you are following God's will. They aren't.

"A man who wanders out of the way of understanding shall abide in the congregation of the spirits (of the dead)." Proverbs 21:16

Genocide of Millions of Christians

Between the 13th and 19th centuries (600 years) the Roman Catholic religion Inquisitions executed up to 9 million people (Wikipedia). 10's of millions more were massacred by Rome for the crime of "heresy" by those they classified as "dissident" Christians in the French wars (1562-1598), The Thirty Years war in Europe (1618-1648) and following the start of the Protestant Reformation (1517), to name a few.

The Roman Catholic religion currently has 1.4 billion global members.

This pales in comparison to 1400 years of the Islamic religion who revel in their global terrorism and atrocities, responsible for the slaughtering of millions of Christians, just because they're Christian, including women, children and babies.

"More than 365 MILLION Christians face genocide." Gatestone Institute 2024

"Islam is the main culprit." World Watch List 2024

Each Muslim and Muslim sympathizer (e.g. government, corporation, education system, mongrel Christian, etc.) is a génocidaire or genocider, guilty by allegiance to or acceptance of this religion that commands the killing of unbelievers.

Every nation, government, religion, education system, media and entertainment structure, people group and individual become a génocidaire when they consider the Bible to be hate speech because it offends them. Their position fuels the holocaust of innocent people being persecuted, imprisoned, tortured and murdered over it.

Don't follow satan's useful idiots to their eternal doom.

God showing you what not to do and what to do to enter into Heaven is love, not hate. He is love.

"⁷ Beloved, let us love one another, for love is (springs) from God; and he who loves [his fellowmen] is begotten (born) of God and is coming [progressively] to know and understand God [to perceive and recognize and get a better and clearer knowledge of Him].

⁸ He who does not love has not become acquainted with God [does not and never did know Him], for God is love." 1 John 4:7-8

He doesn't want a single person to miss out on Heaven.

Physics, mathematics, biology and chemistry prove that we exist in both a physical and spiritual realm and that the Bible contains reality about existence. Our existence.

God says that everything we think, do, and don't do, affects our lives and eternity. No matter how sweet, noble, politically correct, pious, sincere or violent someone's acts are, it doesn't mean it equals God's Truth or God's Way; it doesn't mean it equals God's definition of love; it doesn't mean you get into Heaven.

CHAPTER 17
"Next"

Exposing religion and those wallowing in it, can sound harsh and unfair, even offensive, judgmental and unloving. Harsh is letting people drop into the lake of fire.

God's love and truth carry certain features that aren't usually discussed in religious circles. God wants people to snap out of their religious fog. He doesn't want anyone to be misled, cursed or lost forever from Him.

He wants you to desire Him and love Him as He desires and loves you. He willingly and freely offers everyone love, mercy, grace, forgiveness, and peace that surpasses all understanding, treasures, rulership, power, and authority, but He can't defy His Word. Religions lead people down wrong paths when they ignore God's Word, such as sin, repentance, discipline, abomination, justice, and judgment.

They think God will just give everyone a free pass or that He'll accept their "magic ticket." We need to follow His entire way, not mongrelize or "cherry-pick" just some of our personal favorites.

All should keep in mind, that one day, each of us is going to hear a word ring out; the word "Next!"

An angel will escort you up to your place of judgment.

"^{36} But I tell you, on the day of judgment men will have to give account for every idle (inoperative, nonworking) word they speak.

^{37} For by your words you will be justified and acquitted, and by your words you will be condemned and sentenced." Matthew 12:36-37

Then the book of life will be opened.

"^{11} Then I saw a great white throne and the One Who was seated upon it, from Whose presence and from the sight of Whose face earth and sky fled away, and no place was found for them.

^{12} I [also] saw the dead, great and small; they stood before the throne, and books were opened. Then another book was opened, which is [the Book] of Life. And the dead were judged (sentenced) by what they had done [their whole way of feeling and acting, their aims and endeavors] in accordance with what was recorded in the books.

^{13} And the sea delivered up the dead who were in it, death and Hades (the state of death or disembodied existence) surrendered the dead in them, and all were tried and their cases determined by what they had done [according to their motives, aims, and works].

¹⁴ Then death and Hades (the state of death or disembodied existence) were thrown into the lake of fire. This is the second death, the lake of fire.

¹⁵ And if anyone's [name] was not found recorded in the Book of Life, he was hurled into the lake of fire." Revelation 20:11-15

Those who accepted and followed the true God, won't fear the word, "Next." We will joyfully race up to God in excitement. We will then receive our full inheritance and all our treasures, as true saints, royal priests, and joint heirs with Christ.

God is waiting for the religious to abandon their ways and accept His Way.

"Take no part in and have no fellowship with the fruitless deeds and enterprises of darkness, but instead [let your lives be so in contrast as to] expose and reprove and convict them." Ephesians 5:11

"⁸ But even if we or an angel from heaven should preach to you a gospel contrary to and different from that which we preached to you, let him be accursed (anathema, devoted to destruction, doomed to eternal punishment)!

⁹ As we said before, so I now say again: If anyone is preaching to you a gospel different from or contrary to that which you received [from us], let him be accursed (anathema, devoted to destruction, doomed to eternal punishment)!" Galatians 1:8-9

"¹⁴ Do not be unequally yoked with unbelievers [do not make mismated alliances with them or come under a different yoke with them, inconsistent with your faith]. For what partnership have right living and right standing with God with iniquity and lawlessness? Or how can light have fellowship with darkness?

¹⁵ What harmony can there be between Christ and Belial [the devil]? Or what has a believer in common with an unbeliever?

¹⁶ What agreement [can there be between] a temple of God and idols? For we are the temple of the living God; even as God said, I will dwell in and with and among them and will walk in and with and among them, and I will be their God, and they shall be My people.

¹⁷ So, come out from among [unbelievers], and separate (sever) yourselves from them, says the Lord, and touch not [any] unclean thing; then I will receive you kindly and treat you with favor,

¹⁸ And I will be a Father to you, and you shall be My sons and daughters, says the Lord Almighty." 2 Corinthians 6:14-18

Believers follow what God says—all of it.

Get off the Wrong Path

If you're on the wrong path, you have some hard decisions to make. I know many who are aware of the truth, yet continue teaching and following an alternate gospel.

Better deal with the hard decisions now as you don't want to wait until you hear, "Next."

Compare what you're doing, believing or being taught against God's Word, the Bible. If your life is built on flesh-driven, religious "bells and whistles" rather than God, then you know what needs to be done.

Religion Conclusion

Humanity has designed their own ideologies, religions, doctrines, laws, philosophies, cults and belief systems throughout history to accommodate their desires or mistaken beliefs. Heaven is closed to them.

"But woe to you, scribes and Pharisees, pretenders (hypocrites)! For you shut the kingdom of heaven in men's faces; for you neither enter yourselves, nor do you allow those who are about to go in to do so." Matthew 23:13

"Heaven [is] My throne, and earth the footstool for My feet. What [kind of] house can you build for Me, says the Lord, or what is the place in which I can rest?" Acts 7:49

"The God Who produced and formed the world and all things in it, being Lord of heaven and earth, does not dwell in handmade shrines." Acts 17:24

"1 For we know that if the tent which is our earthly home is destroyed (dissolved), we have from God a building, a house not made with hands, eternal in the heavens.

2 Here indeed, in this [present abode, body], we sigh and groan inwardly, because we yearn to be clothed over [we yearn to put on our celestial body like a garment, to be fitted out] with our heavenly dwelling." 2 Corinthians 5:1-2

Religion doesn't reflect God's truth.

People have the freedom to think and feel as they like, including about God and Heaven, but, personal ideologies don't equal God's truth or entry into Heaven.

"They profess to know God [to recognize, perceive, and be acquainted with Him], but deny and disown and renounce Him by what they do; they are detestable and loathsome, unbelieving and disobedient and disloyal and rebellious, and [they are] unfit and worthless for good work (deed or enterprise) of any kind." Titus 1:16

"[So], if we say we are partakers together and enjoy fellowship with Him when we live and move and are walking about in darkness, we are [both] speaking falsely and do not live and practice the Truth [which the Gospel presents]." 1 John 1:6

"Whoever says, I know Him [I perceive, recognize, understand, and am acquainted with Him] but fails to keep and obey His commandments (teachings) is a liar, and the Truth [of the Gospel] is not in him." 1 John 2:4

Don't accept anything less than the whole truth.

"A little leaven (a slight inclination to error, or a few false teachers) leavens the whole lump [it perverts the whole conception of faith or misleads the whole church]." Galatians 5:9

SECTION 4

CHAPTER 18
The Stats on Religious Denominations

AFTER LOOKING AT the heretical religious systems, obsolete religious leaders, wolves and zealots, what does statistics say about who in these groups won't make it into Heaven?

World Population claiming to be Christian 31.6% (Wikipedia and Statista)

> Roman Catholic 15.5%
> Protestant 11.4%
> Orthodox 3.7%
> Other <1%

A 31.6% figure of the world that has a chance is shocking enough but it gets worse.

Statistics from the Barna Group reveal that among Roman Catholics, less than one-half of 1% have a Biblical worldview*.

So that's strikes off another 15%.

At the end of the Barna Group research it was determined that only about 4% of people in the world have a Biblical worldview.

Realistically, this figure can be considered much lower if you asked this 4% if they <u>practice</u> Biblical teachings beyond acceptance that all of it is accurate, such as in 1 Corinthians 5:11, "But now I write to you not to associate with anyone who bears the name of [Christian] brother if he is known to be guilty of immorality or greed, or is an idolater [whose soul is devoted to any object that usurps the place of God], or is a person with a foul tongue [railing, abusing, reviling, slandering], or is a drunkard or a swindler or a robber. [No] you must not so much as eat with such a person."

A mongrelized, quasi-Christian or cultural-Christianity mindset doesn't get a pass from God. There's more involved than wearing a cross, owning a Bible, attending "church" and speaking Christianese.

Take a hard look at where you are before it's too late, as following herds of lemmings over a cliff, because 95%+ of people are going that way so it must be right, is not a survivable solution.

*"For the purposes of the research, a Biblical worldview was defined as believing that absolute moral truths exist; that such truth is defined by the Bible; and firm belief in six specific religious views. Those views were that Jesus Christ lived a sinless life; God is the all-powerful and all-knowing Creator of the universe and He stills rules it today; salvation is a gift from God and cannot be earned; Satan is real; a Christian has a responsibility to share their faith in Christ with other people; and the Bible is accurate in all of its teachings." Barna Group

CHAPTER 19
Infidels and Heretics

Let's dig into mongrels a little more now.

Infidels and heretics trick even the highly intelligent into spending eternity outside of Heaven with them and the devil in the lake of fire.

"For false Christs and false prophets will arise, and they will show great signs and wonders so as to deceive and lead astray, if possible, even the elect (God's chosen ones)." Matthew 24:24

The true definition of an infidel is one who follows another religion/doesn't believe in or follow God's reality, considered antichrist (i.e. Buddhism, Hinduism, Judaism, Islamism, etc.).

Remember, "Do not be unequally yoked with unbelievers [do not make mismated alliances with them or come under a different yoke with them, inconsistent with your faith]. For what partnership have right living and right standing with God with iniquity and lawlessness? Or how can light have fellowship with darkness?" 2 Corinthians 6:14

We've touched on the heretics who follow material that ignores, contradicts or compromises with the Word of God.

Most proclaimed Christians are cessationist (i.e. Anglican, Baptist, Lutheran, Presbyterian), meaning they believe God's power ceased at the end of the Apostolic Age or death of the last of the twelve disciples.

They contradict the Bible in this belief as others performed miracles besides the twelve disciples.

"And God did unusual and extraordinary miracles by the hands of Paul." Acts 19:11. See also about the 70 others Jesus sent out in Luke 10:1-17 who healed and cast out demons and Stephen Acts 6:8. The internet has countless examples of God's miracles over the last 2000-year history to present day, performed by what many refer to as mystics and others, including bilocation, instant healing, raising the dead, etc. We discussed a few in Chapter 7. This isn't magic. It's God. Giving credit to satan for counterfeiting God's power is blasphemy. Saying the Holy Spirit stopped being God 2000 years ago and doesn't operate in believers anymore is heresy.

"Do you not know that your body is the temple (the very sanctuary) of the Holy Spirit Who lives within you, Whom you have received [as a Gift] from God? You are not your own." 1 Corinthians 6:19

Be careful not to be corrupt or a heretic, as even those with God's power, Jesus warned in Matthew 7:22-24, "²² Many will say to Me on that day*, Lord, Lord, have we not prophesied in Your name and driven out demons in Your name and done many mighty works in Your name?

²³ And then I will say to them openly (publicly), I never knew you; depart from Me, you who act wickedly [disregarding My commands].

²⁴ So everyone who hears these words of Mine and acts upon them [obeying them] will be like a sensible (prudent, practical, wise) man who built his house upon the rock."

*Their judgment day

People don't want to hear about infidels and heretics. They sound like some medieval words that aren't valid anymore. Satan loves it when people think that.

Unfortunately, infidels and heretics are words that you'll probably never hear (I never did) at gatherings.

INFIDELS AND HERETICS

Enlightened Ilk AKA Forerunners

Some "enlightened" leaders today or "forerunners," tell foolish listeners that the church-age is dead (I forget what age they proclaim we're in now as it changes it seems monthly).

They say they've discovered new "absolutes" now that everyone should be doing, while contradicting some of God's basic "absolutes" for <u>survival</u> (getting into Heaven). Some of this ilk have CD's/DVD's/books/international supernatural schools/podcasts/webinars/YouTube sites/media, telling paying followers such heretical lies like you can go to hell in the spirit and release the dead or that satan will one day be redeemed and go to Heaven with everyone else who died, because God is too loving to leave them in the lake of fire. They attract with their enthralling spiritual testimonies that they mix with nonsense that removes Jesus as Savior and the Gospel of its truth.

Heresy Shifts with Invention

Each religion and their subsets have their own false definitions of infidel or heretic, which they would say is anyone who follows a different doctrine than the ones they've invented.

For instance, as mentioned, the Roman Catholic religious crowd conducted inquisitions for centuries, imprisoning, putting people to death and going to war for those daring to oppose the numerous heretical doctrines made up by their popes. False doctrines that they still follow today.

"³ For the time is coming when [people] will not tolerate (endure) sound and wholesome instruction, but, having ears itching [for something pleasing and gratifying], they will gather to themselves one teacher after another to a considerable number, chosen to satisfy their own liking and to foster the errors they hold,

⁴ And will turn aside from hearing the truth and wander off into myths and man-made fictions." 2 Timothy 4:3-4

Simply put, the Bible is God's Word. Anything that contradicts it or compromises with it is heresy.

Paul said, "¹¹ For I want you to know, brethren, that the Gospel which was proclaimed and made known by me is not man's gospel [a human invention, according to or patterned after any human standard].

¹² For indeed I did not receive it from man, nor was I taught it, but [it came to me] through a [direct] revelation [given] by Jesus Christ (the Messiah)." Galatians 1:11-12

There isn't enough paper to list all the heretical doctrines adopted by the thousands of groups in the world. It's up to you to research into whatever or whoever it is you follow to match it against God's truth.

Many would say to a heresy label, "So what if I'm not perfect. We all sin. I'm covered by grace, mercy and the Blood. Once saved, always saved. Blah blah (fill in the blank)."

Any and all justification people dream up for their heresy doesn't change that they're a heretic that God says are cursed.

"⁷ Not that there is [or could be] any other [genuine Gospel], but there are [obviously] some who are troubling and disturbing and bewildering you [with a different kind of teaching which they offer as a gospel] and want to pervert and distort the Gospel of Christ (the Messiah) [into something which it absolutely is not].

⁸ But even if we or an angel from heaven should preach to you a gospel contrary to and different from that which we preached to you, let him be accursed (anathema, devoted to destruction, doomed to eternal punishment)!

⁹ As we said before, so I now say again: If anyone is preaching to you a gospel different from or contrary to that which you received [from us], let him be accursed (anathema, devoted to destruction, doomed to eternal punishment)!" Galatians 1:7-9

Wake Up Call

The goal here is not to condemn, as God has already done that for the infidels and the heretics. The goal here is a wake-up call to those who will take God seriously about their eternal life.

"¹⁷ I appeal to you, brethren, to be on your guard concerning those who create dissensions and difficulties and cause divisions, in opposition to the doctrine (the teaching) which you have been taught. [I warn you to turn aside from them, to] avoid them.

¹⁸ For such persons do not serve our Lord Christ but their own appetites and base desires, and by ingratiating and flattering speech, they beguile the hearts of the unsuspecting and simpleminded [people]." Romans 16:17-18

"But refuse and avoid irreverent legends (profane and impure and godless fictions, mere grandmothers' tales) and silly myths, and express your disapproval of them. Train yourself toward godliness (piety), [keeping yourself spiritually fit]." 1 Timothy 4:7

God says, we are to avoid infidels and heretics and expose them.

Heretical Doubletalk

Those who tell me that they aren't personally heretical, but they don't avoid or expose heretics they follow or listen to, are still heretics as they contradict God's Word for them. See how that works? They say something like, "Well, this teacher has a lot of good stuff even though I know that that small part they say is heresy. I eat the meat and toss the bones. Blah, blah (fill in the blank)." Still heresy. You're giving them a corrupted trading floor or platform in your life as well as you're showing others that you accept heretics when you don't avoid and expose them, according to God's Word. You never want to lead others to heretical teachers you follow, as this makes you a heretical teacher.

Bears repeating...

"⁶ [About the condition of your church] your boasting is not good [indeed, it is most unseemly and entirely out of place]. Do you not know that [just] a little leaven will ferment the whole lump [of dough]?

⁷ Purge (clean out) the old leaven that you may be fresh (new) dough, still uncontaminated [as you are], for Christ, our Passover [Lamb], has been sacrificed." 1 Corinthians 5:6-7

"A little leaven (a slight inclination to error, or a few false teachers) leavens the whole lump [it perverts the whole conception of faith or misleads the whole church]." Galatians 5:9

Those who teach heresy will have a special punishment.

We covered in Chapter 14 on God's position on false leaders (e.g. 2 Peter 2) their heresies, their fate and the fate of those who follow them.

Cut 'em Lose

I asked a former acquaintance why he associated with a group that had some obvious heretical doctrines. He said it was the best he could find. I told him that's not a God standard. He continued his association with them so, following God's Word to avoid heretics, I then disassociated myself with him.

Other leaders have told me they don't condemn sin or heresy in others, they just love them. You're not loving people by letting them stay on the road to the lake of fire. That's taking part in spiritual genocide. You're also seriously harming yourself when you run your own show contrary to what God says you should be doing… in this instance, not avoiding or acceptance of infidels and heretics.

God's Word is talking to all in the world who want to walk with Him now and through eternity, on what to do/or not do to be successful or what to do/or not do to be cursed.

None of what I'm pointing out here are my theories, conjectures nor opinions. Take God at His Word.

Quick Heresy Checklist

We all have to guard our thoughts, words and actions to avoid heresy. Repent when you fall into heresy, learn from it, don't repeat it, successfully move forward with God.

To recap:

- Never follow a man-made, different Gospel Romans 16:17-18; Galatians 1:7-9; 11-12; 2 Timothy 4:3-4
- Avoid those who teach heresy, contra-God's Word, even if it's just one thing (a little leaven), which pollutes you and others who follow your lead Romans 16:17-18; 1 Timothy 4:7; Ephesians 5:11; 1 Corinthians 5:6; Galatians 5:9
- Expose those who teach heresy, even if it's just one thing (a little leaven), which pollutes you and others who follow them 1 Timothy 4:7; Ephesians 5:11
- Don't operate in flesh mindsets, but with the Holy Spirit Romans 8:8; 14
- Never, ever teach heresy 2 Peter 2

Check what you believe, who you listen to, who you associate with, against what God says in His Word.

Once you're on the right path with God, under the guidance and power of the Holy Spirit, reveal the pitfalls of and condemn heresy to warn and correct people. As a watchman this is a requirement to save others and save yourself.

"⁸ When I say to the wicked, O wicked man, you shall surely die, and you do not speak to warn the wicked from his way, that wicked man shall die in his perversity and iniquity, but his blood will I require at your hand.

[9] But if you warn the wicked to turn from his evil way and he does not turn from his evil way, he shall die in his iniquity, but you will have saved your life." Ezekiel 33:8-9

Decisions on associating with infidels and heretics close to you will usually be made easy as they'll either ignore you, cast you out from their midst or attack you (verbally and/or physically).

You'll probably soon discover that it's safer and more peaceful to walk alone with God as a saint, true child of God, royal priest and joint-heir with Christ, than be aligned with any infidels or heretical leaders, groups, friends or family, as God says, they will destroy your life.

Guard your eternity.

CHAPTER 20
Who Else Does God say won't get into Heaven?

LET'S EXAMINE SOME of God's specific examples of fools, infidels and heretics.

"⁹ Do you not know that the unrighteous and the wrongdoers will not inherit or have any share in the kingdom of God? Do not be deceived (misled): neither the impure and immoral, nor idolaters, nor adulterers, nor those who participate in homosexuality,

¹⁰ Nor cheats (swindlers and thieves), nor greedy graspers, nor drunkards, nor foulmouthed revilers and slanderers, nor extortioners and robbers will inherit or have any share in the kingdom of God." 1 Corinthians 6:9-10

⁹ Do you not know that the unrighteous will not inherit the kingdom of God? Do not be deceived. Neither fornicators, nor idolaters, nor adulterers, nor homosexuals, nor sodomites,

¹⁰ nor thieves, nor covetous, nor drunkards, nor revilers, nor extortioners will inherit the kingdom of God." 1 Corinthians 6:9-10 NKJV

¹⁸ Shun immorality and all sexual looseness [flee from impurity in thought, word, or deed]. Any other sin which a man commits is one outside the body, but he who commits sexual immorality sins against his own body." 1 Corinthians 6:18

"²¹ Not everyone who says to Me, Lord, Lord, will enter the kingdom of heaven, but he who does the will of My Father Who is in heaven.

²² Many will say to Me on that day, Lord, Lord, have we not prophesied in Your name and driven out demons in Your name and done many mighty works in Your name?

²³ And then I will say to them openly (publicly), I never knew you; depart from Me, you who act wickedly [disregarding My commands]." Matthew 7:21-23

¹⁹ Now the doings (practices) of the flesh are clear (obvious): they are immorality, impurity, indecency,

²⁰ Idolatry, sorcery, enmity, strife, jealousy, anger (ill temper), selfishness, divisions (dissensions), party spirit (factions, sects with peculiar opinions, heresies),

²¹ Envy, drunkenness, carousing, and the like. I warn you beforehand, just as I did previously, that those who do such things shall not inherit the kingdom of God." Galatians 5:19-21

⁵ For be sure of this: that no person practicing sexual vice or impurity in thought or in life, or one who is covetous [who has lustful desire for the property of others and is greedy for gain]—for he [in effect] is an idolater—has any inheritance in the kingdom of Christ and of God." Ephesians 5:5

⁸ But as for the cowards and the ignoble and the contemptible and the cravenly lacking in courage and the cowardly submissive, and as for the unbelieving and faithless, and as for the depraved and defiled with abominations, and as for murderers and the lewd and adulterous and the practicers of magic arts and the idolaters (those who give supreme devotion to anyone or anything other than God) and all liars (those who knowingly convey untruth by word or deed)—[all of these shall have] their part in the lake that blazes with fire and brimstone. This is the second death." Revelation 21:8

"¹² But what I do, I will continue to do, [for I am determined to maintain this independence] in order to cut off the claim of those who would like [to find an occasion and incentive] to claim that in their boasted [mission] they work on the same terms that we do.

¹³ For such men are false apostles [spurious, counterfeits], deceitful workmen, masquerading as apostles (special messengers) of Christ (the Messiah).

¹⁴ And it is no wonder, for Satan himself masquerades as an angel of light;

¹⁵ So it is not surprising if his servants also masquerade as ministers of righteousness. [But] their end will correspond with their deeds." 2 Corinthians 11:12-15

The list of those that GOD says don't get into Heaven

Adulterers
Anger
Anti-Christ
Blasphemers
Carousing
Cheats, Greedy Graspers, Extortioners, Robbers, Thieves
Cowards and the ignoble
Depraved and defiled with abominations
Divisions
Drunkenness
Enmity
Envy
Faithless

False apostles, deceitful workers (in roles as pope, priests, pastors, leaders)
Fornicators
Foul-mothed Revilers
Heretics
Homosexuals
Idolaters
Immoral
Impure in Thought or Life
Indecency
Infidels
Jealousy
Liars
Murderers
Party spirit (heresy)
Practicers of magic arts
Selfishness
Sexual Immorality
Sinners
Slanderers
Sodomites
Sorcery
Strife
Those who act wickedly (disregard God's commands)
Unbelieving
Unforgiveness
Unrepentant
Unrighteous
Wrongdoers

HOW TO GET INTO HEAVEN... GUARANTEED

How many of the 4% in that Barna Group survey we covered are on this list? How many land in multiple spots?

Make sure you don't make this list.

Repent if and when you do.

CHAPTER 21
Can a Person Lose Salvation?

Once Saved, Always Saved?

ONE OF THE main false doctrines that trap the unsuspecting is the "once saved, always saved" or "eternal security" doctrine believed by millions in many denominations (Baptist, Calvary Chapel, Messianic Judaism, Presbyterian) to be Biblical fact.

It's a death trap.

There are roughly 113 biblical scripture teachings indicating that a person can lose salvation.

The false doctrine of "once saved, always saved" is the belief that once an individual has been genuinely saved through accepting Jesus Christ as their Savior, they cannot, under any circumstances, lose their salvation.

They're professing, they're eternally secure because all of their sins, both past <u>and</u> future, have been forgiven. This, in effect, is a belief that once someone has been saved, they can fall into sin of any sort, deliberate and non-deliberate, and still be saved.

According to them, once a person is saved, continuing in sin, such as adultery or fornication, even murder is absolved, as they remain saved through grace.

What does the Bible say about this?

Jesus Christ brought us the New Covenant and, like all covenants, conditions must be met <u>if</u> the benefits are to be received. Throughout the New Testament, the word <u>'if'</u> is used many times in association with salvation. When the conditions God sets by these 'ifs' are not met then an individual can't expect to receive the rewards, as God never makes idle claims.

The Conditional Word 'If'

Romans 8:12-14 clearly state that God's children have an obligation to keep from <u>sin</u>, through the power of the <u>Holy Spirit</u>, and the penalty for not doing so is death.

"¹² So then, brethren, we are debtors, but not to the flesh [we are not obligated to our carnal nature], to live [a life ruled by the standards set up by the dictates] of the flesh.

¹³ For if you live according to [the dictates of] the flesh, you will surely die. But if through the power of the [Holy] Spirit you

are [habitually] putting to death (making extinct, deadening) the [evil] deeds prompted by the body, you shall [really and genuinely] live forever.

¹⁴ For all who are led by the Spirit of God are sons of God."

The following verses use the conditional word 'if' regarding salvation:

* 1 Corinthians 15:2 says that we are saved only if we hold to the Word
* Hebrews 3:6 says we are of God's house if we hold fast
* Hebrews 3:14 says we are partakers of Christ if we are steadfast to the end
* Hebrews 10:36-39 says that if the righteous (just) draw back they face destruction (lake of fire)

There is a conditional 'if' associated with salvation in each of these verses. In each case, believers must fulfill the condition in order to receive the promised reward. The condition is perseverance and the reward is eternal life.

Hebrews 10:26-31 says there are 7 ways to lose salvation:

1. Willfully sinning
2. Renounce Christ as the <u>only</u> sacrifice
3. Despise the Gospel
4. Tread the Son of God under our feet
5. Count Christ's Blood as an unholy thing

6. Despise or blaspheme the Holy Spirit
7. Become an adversary of Christ

How many Christians willfully sin?

How many Christians accept only the parts of the Gospel that fit their religion and come against Christians who follow all of the Gospel?

How many Christians accept other religions and philosophies and mix it with the <u>only</u> sacrifice and the <u>only</u> Gospel acceptable to God the Father?

Some may ask, what about apostasy or sinning with the <u>expectation</u> or <u>acceptance</u> of their church?

Many leaders participate in, accept and/or expect certain activities that God considers sin, in <u>their</u> doctrinal belief that it is not really sinning. Even though The Bible clearly states, that actions such as idol worship, homosexuality and fornication is abhorrent to God <u>and leads to death</u>. (Romans 1:21-31; 1 Corinthians 6:9-10)

Leaders who teach, practice and allow such activities, are taking themselves and others to spiritual death and will have much to account for from God at their judgment.

Each person will be held accountable for <u>their</u> life and what they did with it.

Many also think that they can do whatever they want and just repent afterwards, confess to a priest, pay an offering and say a few prayers and all is well to continue with their willful sins.

God isn't a fool.

Reconciled, Grace and Perseverance

If an individual is reconciled, it means they were saved, lost it and then came back to salvation.

The following verses speak of such individuals, who have subsequently fallen, or can fall, from their position in the Lord.

Colossians 1:21-23 says, "And although you at one time were estranged and alienated from Him and were of hostile attitude of mind in your wicked activities, Yet now has [Christ, the Messiah] reconciled [you to God] in the body of His flesh through death, in order to present you holy and faultless and irreproachable in His [the Father's] presence [And this He will do] provided that you continue to stay with and in the faith [in Christ], well-grounded and settled and steadfast, not shifting or moving away from the hope [which rests on and is inspired by] the glad tidings (the Gospel)…"

Reconciled means returning to being right with God.

Hebrews 10:26-29 briefly says "If we deliberately keep on sinning after we have received the knowledge of the truth, no sacrifice for sins is left, but only a fearful expectation of judgment and of raging fire ... a man deserves to be punished ... who has treated as an unholy thing the blood of the covenant that sanctified him ..."

People here are warned that they can face judgment, even after having been 'sanctified by the blood.'

Sanctification follows justification so the individuals alluded to here have been saved.

If we fail to repent of our sin, to be cleansed by the blood of Jesus, then our heart will harden against the Holy Spirit's conviction.

It will get more and more difficult to bring to the Lord for cleansing, and may lead to eventual salvation loss.

Grace

Some teach that a saved person is covered by grace, yet God's Word says a person can fall from His grace.

Galatians 5:4 says, "If you seek to be justified and declared righteous and to be given a right standing with God through the Law, you are brought to nothing and so separated (severed) from Christ. You have fallen away from grace (from God's gracious favor and unmerited blessing)."

The Jews spoken of here, having reverted to the Law of Moses, have been alienated from the Lord; they have fallen from grace.

Obviously, they were once 'in Grace,' that is, they were once saved.

Perseverance

Perseverance in faith is required to reap the benefits of God's promises.

Romans 2:6-7 says that eternal life is the reward for the saint's perseverance (patient continuance). Hebrews 10:36 says we need to persevere to receive God's promises. Revelation 14:12 speaks of perseverance. 1 Timothy 4:16 tells Timothy to persevere to save himself.

Once again, in Romans 8:12-14, Paul gives clear warning to his brothers in Christ. This passage says that we are debtors and have an obligation to steadfastly keep from sin by the power of the Holy Spirit, otherwise we shall die. Verse 14 speaks of being 'led' by the Holy Spirit. Being led doesn't mean that the Holy Spirit has us on a leash but that we voluntarily follow His leading. It's our responsibility to live by the Spirit otherwise we will die... be lost.

Also in Galatians 6:7-8 and Galatians 5:19-21 Paul is warning believers, for the second time, that they must live Godly lives if they wish to inherit the kingdom of God.

There is no doubt that we have assurance of salvation because of verses such as 1 John 5:13 and Jude 1:24 as well as the witness of the Spirit, however, we have a part to play in persevering.

Persevering in faith is not works, otherwise the confession and repentance required of us to be saved initially would also be works.

Our initial trusting to be saved and the ongoing perseverance required of us are an <u>internal</u> 'work' of the heart and mind (Note John 6:29 regarding the work of God).

We are continually urged to keep from sin, to walk in the Spirit, to persevere in faith and so remain in Jesus.

Romans 8:35-39 says that nothing in creation can separate us from <u>God's love</u>, neither famine, sword, angels nor demons etc. These things are all <u>external</u> to us and things over which we have no control.

God promises to keep us through these trials as clearly stated in Hebrews 13:5-6. However, these verses don't speak of the <u>internal</u> perseverance (our control of our will) required to walk in holiness through the Holy Ghost/Spirit. We have freedom of will to do this. God never controls our will. He helps us to persevere.

"[Not in your own strength] for it is God Who is all the while effectually at work in you [energizing and creating in you the power and desire], both to will and to work for His good pleasure and satisfaction and delight." Philippians 2:13.

The Failure to Persevere will Bring Judgment

Hebrews 6:4-6 speaks of people being unable to be brought back (renewed again) to repentance. They were clearly saved at one stage as they shared in the Holy Spirit who only dwells in believers, as stated in Act 5:32. To be brought back to repentance can only mean that they had been repentant in the first place. You can't be brought back to a place that you have never been to, you can only be brought 'to' that place.

2 Peter 2:20-22 tells us of people facing judgment after having once known Jesus. They had escaped the pollution of the world through knowledge of Jesus (2 Peter 1:3), but have returned to the mire. If they are going <u>back</u>, then they must have left it in the first place. Only Jesus could have initially saved them from the corruption of the world to which they have returned, as Romans 8:7 makes clear.

In Matthew 5:13 Jesus tells his disciples, who are the salt of the earth, that if they lose their saltiness they will be cast out.

Only the saved are disciples of Jesus and He warned them against going back into the world.

John 15:6 speaks of branches cast into the fire because they failed to abide. Only a saved person is a branch in the Vine.

In Matthew 10:32-33 Jesus tells the disciples that He will deny (disown) them if they deny Him. This is repeated in 2 Timothy 2:12-13 where Paul says that if we endure (suffer) then we will reign with the Lord, but if we deny Him, He will deny us.

Other Verses Showing the Possibility of Salvation Loss

2 Peter 3:17 urges us to take care of the secure position from which we can fall. The onus is on us.

There would be no care about falling, nothing to guard against, if we go to Heaven no matter what we do.

James 5:19-20 speaks of a brother becoming a sinner and being brought back to repentance, saving him from death.

A human effort is involved here. God puts the responsibility on man.

The prodigal son, in Luke 15, is an example of this; he had died (spiritually) and was made alive again, saving him from death.

Hebrews 3:12-14 warns brothers not to turn from the living God but to hold firmly till the end.

Even Timothy is warned to watch himself and persevere in his life and doctrine to ensure his salvation (1 Timothy 4:16).

In 1 Corinthians 9:27 and 2 Timothy 4:7 Paul speaks of his efforts, fighting the good fight and keeping the faith, so that he wouldn't be castaway.

Some Objections Answered

In Ephesians 5:18, we are told to be filled with the Holy Spirit.

From the Greek text, the word 'filled' is better translated 'continue to be filled.'

Likewise, 'believe' in John 3:16 has a similar tense, meaning that we need to 'continue to believe' or 'go on believing' in order to receive eternal life.

In other words, we must persevere in believing.

Jesus made this obvious in John 15:6 when He said, "If anyone does not remain in me, he is like a branch that is thrown away and withers; such branches are picked up, thrown into the fire and burned." NIV

In John 10:27-28 Jesus promises to protect those who hear <u>and</u> follow Him. Following requires an effort of will, it's not automatic.

The verses speak directly of Jesus' power to protect the believer against <u>anyone or any man</u> plucking a disciple from His hand. He doesn't say that an individual can't leave of their own free will but that no person can snatch them from His hand.

Jude 1:24 only tells us that Jesus is <u>able</u> to keep us from falling, not that He <u>will</u>, regardless of our actions.

Regarding being sealed with the Spirit: Scripture plainly says that the Holy Spirit is given to us as a witness and a guarantee of our salvation until the day of redemption... Ephesians 1:13-14 & Romans 8:16.

His Presence convicts us of sin, leading us to repentance and holy living... Romans 8:3-4 and Titus 3:4-8. However, Scripture also plainly says that if we fail to co-operate with the Holy Spirit we will be lost ... Romans 8:12-13.

Be Sure

The 'ifs' in many verses and the simplicity of verses such as John 15:6 and Matthew 5:13 cannot simply be ignored.

Like the Israelites of old, obedience (<u>following</u> God's laws) is required to reap the benefits of a promise as stated in Isaiah 1:19 -20. Note the clear warning, to the righteous, in Ezekiel 33:12-13.

We are saved by Grace, through faith and to remain saved we must persevere in that faith to be kept from deliberate, ongoing sin or face a Christless eternity.

No one can live a sinless life but we must be kept from the type of sins which are listed in Galatians 5:19-21.

1 John 2:1-2 says that we shouldn't sin but if we do, we are to take it to Jesus in repentance and He will forgive us and cleanse us of it as stated in 1 John 1:9.

The word 'if' in this verse is critical... if we don't confess, we won't be forgiven.

The choice is ours.

If you have any apostasy or unconfessed sins, repent to God in heartfelt repentance. Get rid of them.

He's waiting.

Jesus said, "the one who stands firm to the end will be saved." Mark 13:13

Don't be deceived.

Don't leave the most important factor of your life to chance or dependence on mongrelized or fantasy ideology/doctrines.

Be sure.

CHAPTER 22
Sin

SIN CAN BE actions, inactions and thoughts that God (Bible), not man, says will keep you out of Heaven.

Declaring that you don't sin or sins are covered by grace is a deceived path, as God says we need to recognize our sins, be sorrowful about them and repent/turn away from them.

Each person must go through their own life to see what sins they've committed and deal with them as the main goal is to ensure that you get into Heaven.

Analyzing all possible sin would be exhaustive so we'll just examine one area that people habitually and blindly partake in that God hates and considers to be an abomination.

Lying

Lying jeopardizes a person's relationship with God and their survival.

"By age four, 90% of children have grasped the concept of lying". *University of Massachusetts*

According to a 2002 study conducted by the *University of Massachusetts*... "60% of adults can't have a ten-minute conversation without lying at least once. But even that number makes it sound better than it really is; those people in the study who did lie actually told an average of 3 lies during their brief chat. And I know you're sitting there right now insisting you would be part of the 40% that didn't lie. That's what the liars in the study thought, too. When they watched the taped conversations back, they were shocked at how many fibs they had told."

"According to *The Day America Told the Truth*, 86% of us are lying to our parents regularly, followed by friends (75%), siblings (73%), and spouses (69%)."

"30% of internet users are looking for love on a dating site. According to a study by *Scientific American*, a whopping 90% of people looking for a date online lie in their profile."

"40% of people lie on their resumes."

"6 times- The average number of lies per day by men to their partner, boss, or colleagues."

"3 times- The average number of lies per day by women to their partner, boss, or colleagues." *StatisticBrain*

These are just a few statistics from the internet.

Wikipedia estimates in 2021 says about 63% of Americans identify as Christian (and 31.6% in the world), so these high percentages of liars include those who consider themselves Christian.

How about false teachers and prophets who make up prophecies for fame and profit and to manipulate people?

God says, "But the prophet who presumes to speak a word in My name which I have not commanded him to speak, or who speaks in the name of other gods, that same prophet shall die." Deuteronomy 18: 20

I know of a "sister act" where one stood up in "church" to give false tongues, with her sister standing up to "interpret." They would decide in advance what they were going to say in order to manipulate and control the leadership and people to do what they wanted. Their false ministry of lies was uncovered, but not after much damage had been done.

I've heard many testimonies over the years of wolves (Christian witchcraft) being exposed who were in leadership positions as Sunday school teachers, worship leaders, youth pastors, prayer teams, etc. in deliberate plots to destroy people.

There are many leaders, even internationally recognized ones, who lie to people and have personal agendas in order to obtain power and wealth. They tell people anything to get them to support them and buy their books, CD's and DVD's.

"Securing treasures by a lying tongue is a vapor driven to and fro; those who seek them seek death." Proverbs 21:6

Pagan Rituals

Then there are the Christians all over the world that celebrate Easter and Christmas (and Halloween), which are lies built on pagan rituals (the truth is easily accessible). Even when the truth is revealed to people, I know very few who have abandoned these lies. Tradition, social pressure and indifference enforce these lies in them.

Christians tell their kids there's a tooth-fairy, leprechauns, Santa Claus and an Easter bunny, knowing full well that these are all deliberate lies.

People will admit that they see no problem in lying to be polite or diplomatic, thinking that these kinds of lies are justified, as they don't hurt anyone and say that they can be helpful.

"[16] These six things the Lord hates, indeed, seven are an abomination to Him:

¹⁷ A proud look [the spirit that makes one overestimate himself and underestimate others], a lying tongue, and hands that shed innocent blood,

¹⁸ A heart that manufactures wicked thoughts and plans, feet that are swift in running to evil,

¹⁹ A false witness who breathes out lies [even under oath], and he who sows discord among his brethren."

God's condemnation of lying here in Proverbs 6:16–19 contains no exception clause to lying or that certain lies are acceptable. Note that 2 of the 7 things God hates is lying.

Lying is high on His list of abominations.

The glaring difference between lies by Christians and lies by non-believers is that Christians also have lies and deceit as doctrine on an organizational level. Religious organization's lie, compromise with God's Word and/or ignore parts of God's Word (which is deliberately withholding the truth or lying). A few examples: the rise of chrislam (Islam acceptance by Christian denominations); acceptance of sexual immorality; idolatry (i.e. praying to/revering physical objects and the dead); lying to people about salvation (i.e. once saved, always saved false doctrine and/or salvation by works i.e. through good deeds or by giving money to the "church" or the false doctrine of salvation through a priest or a particular religion/organization).

It's easy to identify lies within an organization (i.e. false church/ministry/school), when you compare them to what they say and how they act compared to what God says is the truth.

Lying includes all the many cute phraseologies people use such as half-truths, white-lies, fibs, bending the truth, cherry-picking (from God's Word), compromising (with God's Word), withholding the truth, and deception.

One of the worst lies that I've run into, are Christians who won't confront, rebuke, renounce or stop associating with liars (and deliberate, unrepentant sinners), reasoning that we should just love them, and not judge them.

Acceptance of sin breeds more sin, as we can see from the abysmal state of the "church" and the world today. God's people should be a beacon of truth, life and hope to the world. God provides commands on how we are to deal with the rebellious.

"See to it that no one carries you off as spoil or makes you yourselves captive by his so-called philosophy and intellectualism and vain deceit (idle fancies and plain nonsense), following human tradition (men's ideas of the material rather than the spiritual world), just crude notions following the rudimentary and elemental teachings of the universe and disregarding [the teachings of] Christ (the Messiah)." Colossians 2:8

The sin of lying on its own destroys billions of people.

Sure, telling the truth isn't always easy; in fact, it can be extremely tough to do at times. But God calls us to be truth-tellers. Being truthful is precious to God (Proverbs 12:22); it demonstrates the fear of Lord. Furthermore, to tell the truth is not a suggestion, it's a command (Psalm 15:2; Zechariah 8:16; Ephesians 4:25). Being truthful flies in the face of satan, the "father of lies" (John 8:44). Being truthful honors the Lord, who is the "God of truth" (Psalm 31:5, ISV). Lying invites and attracts evil spirits into your life; truth resists and repels them (James 4:7).

"A false witness shall not be unpunished, and he who breathes forth lies shall perish." Proverbs 19: 9

"Whoever says, I know Him [I perceive, recognize, understand, and am acquainted with Him] but fails to keep and obey His commandments (teachings) is a liar, and the Truth [of the Gospel] is not in him." 1 John 2: 4

"But as for the cowards and the ignoble and the contemptible and the cravenly lacking in courage and the cowardly submissive, and as for the unbelieving and faithless, and as for the depraved and defiled with abominations, and as for murderers and the lewd and adulterous and the practicers of magic arts and the idolaters (those who give supreme devotion to anyone or anything other than God) and <u>all liars</u> (those who knowingly convey untruth by word or deed)—[all of these shall have] their part in the lake that blazes with fire and brimstone. This is the second death." Revelation 21: 8

We've all lied in our lives, but the key is to recognize this sin, repent, operate in the truth and reject liars and all doctrines of lies. Survival depends on it.

Recognizing all sin in our life would be impossible considering the number of sins, including thought sin and sins we wouldn't suspect of being sin such as jealousy or gossiping (Romans 1:29). Repent and turn away from those sins that you know of and study what God considers sin so you stay clear of them.

At least once a day consider sincerely repenting of all known sin and those you may have ignorantly fallen into.

Save lives… teach God's Truth to others.

CHAPTER 23
Forgiveness

O<small>NE OF THE</small> main hindrances that can block you from Heaven is unforgiveness.

You must seriously address this issue in your life. And, counsel others, especially when they're on their death bed, to make sure they get right with God.

My mom volunteered in palliative care to be with 66 people on their death beds. Lack of forgiveness was a problem with every one of them. When she counselled them on forgiving what people had done to them, they did so and thus, overcame a hindrance to Heaven before it was too late. She of course also counselled them, and their visiting families and friends, on the other HEAVEN'S AXIOMS. This is what saints, royal priests, lords and joint-heirs with Christ do.

"For if you forgive people their trespasses [their reckless and willful sins, leaving them, letting them go, and giving up resentment], your heavenly Father will also forgive you. But if you do not forgive others their trespasses [their reckless and willful sins, leaving them, letting them go, and giving up resentment], neither will your Father forgive you your trespasses." Matthew 6: 14-15

Many people have misconceptions about forgiveness and yet the Bible clearly states that forgiveness takes one, repentance takes one and reconciliation takes two. Many religious people think that to forgive and forget is biblical... to let it go... but there is a process that God requires us to go through.

Forgiveness is Not

Listed below is what forgiveness is <u>not</u>:

Forgiveness is <u>not</u>:

1. Approving of or diminishing sin... such as when people's say, "what's your problem, nobody's perfect" or "everybody makes mistakes so let it go" or "you shouldn't be judgmental" or "it's not a big deal." Such responses come from sinful people who refuse to repent and expect you to accept their sin. It is a big deal... so big that God died for sins that we <u>must</u> repent of in order to get to Heaven. You shouldn't take sins lightly. Don't dishonor the Cross of Jesus or take your or anyone's eternity so lightly.

2. Enabling sin... forgiving people includes confronting and rebuking, which most people don't do. For example... wives misunderstand Bible submission under their hus-

bands when they rebel against the Lord. The submissive wife puts up with it, enabling his sin, which endangers his eternal life, because she wants to be submissive and forgiving.

3. Denying a wrongdoing… people say and act like it didn't happen; or say, "I forgot all about it" or "I didn't let it affect me." Denial of a sin couldn't be further from the truth. Forgiveness is not denial that you were sinned against or that you didn't sin.

4. Waiting for an apology… "I will forgive when they apologize." Some people will never apologize, and/or they will continue in their destructive, foolish ways. Some people will be stubborn, religious and self righteous and they will never confess or admit their wrongdoing. Some people will move away or die and never get a chance to repent to you. So, you forgive them before they apologize.

5. Forgetting… You can't forget those who abused you, mistreated you, abandoned you, neglected you, cheated on you, betrayed you or lied about you. Even when there is forgiveness, repentance and reconciliation, the memory is still there. Perhaps the pain is gone, but totally forgetting sin against you can be impossible. Some quote Jeremiah 31:34, "God will remember their sin no more", saying that we should therefore do the same. God is almighty (we are not) so forgetting by the Blood of Jesus is part of His nature, not ours.

6. Ceasing to feel the pain... Just because it hurts doesn't mean you fail to forgive. Some people had horrible things done to them. It would be cruel to say, "If you've forgiven them, it shouldn't hurt anymore." We don't read in the Bible that all the tears are wiped from our eyes until the resurrection of the dead and the final unveiling of the kingdom. Forgiveness doesn't mean pain free.

7. A onetime event... Is not like you forgive one "small" sin but not the other. Some keep sinning so you need to keep forgiving, regardless of what they have done, if you plan to keep a toxic person in your life.

8. Neglecting justice... You can forgive someone and call the police and have them arrested. You can forgive someone and testify against them in court. The Bible says that we need to obey the government. Even when you have forgiven a person that has committed a crime, they need to reap the consequences of their crime. Forgiving is not neglecting justice. You can forgive and pursue justice.

9. Trusting... For example, if a family member molested you when you were a child and you wonder, should I let them babysit my kids? The answer is, no way. Or my boyfriend hit me and he says, I'm sorry, should we pick of where we left off? The answer is, no way. Or, my spiritual mentor is a heretic, should I continue with them? The answer is, no way. Trust is built slowly and lost quickly. Only those who are naive and gullible would

trust people unconditionally. It takes time to build trust. You need to test relationships before you trust them, even that at various levels. Some of you give your whole heart away but never take it back. Give it slowly, and if someone has sinned against you, trust has to be rebuilt over time, if at all. Some people can be trusted in time after they've bore good fruit in keeping with their repentance and/or they've received professional help. Other people should never be trusted again because the risk is simply too high.

10. Reconciliation… Many think it's Biblical that we must automatically reconcile with those who've sinned against you or wronged you. Many who've sinned, expect things to go "back to normal" with you, as they take what they've done too lightly. It takes one person to repent, it takes one person to forgive and it takes two to reconcile. Paul says in Hebrews 12:14 to make every effort to be at peace with all men, but this doesn't mean reconciliation. Peace may mean that further contact with toxic people be severed. It takes two to reconcile. There are people who have been friends for a long time and one has been hurt by the other but the other person has never sincerely repented. It takes more than just to say, "I'm sorry." You really need to see true repentance and fruit to reconcile. Once trust is broken it's hard to build it back.

We must forgive everyone to receive forgiveness from Father God for our sins, in order to enter into Heaven.

Forgiveness also releases us from the bondage of resentment, bitterness, anger, and hate, which bears fruit of sickness, illness, disease and early death.

Forgiveness is <u>not</u> approving sin, nor enabling sin, nor denying sin, nor waiting for repentance before we forgive, nor forgetting, nor painless, nor selective, nor free of justice, nor trust, nor reconciliation.

Don't let someone else rob you of your inheritance in Heaven because you refuse to forgive them.

CHAPTER 24
Blasphemy

IN THE OLD TESTAMENT blasphemy was a death sentence.

Jewish leaders arrested, tried and had Jesus put to death for blasphemy.

Blasphemy is profane, insulting, disrespect, offensive, sacrilegious talk against God (Father, Jesus and/or The Holy Spirit). Taking the Lord's name in vain. Crediting the things of God to the devil.

"You shall not use or repeat the name of the Lord your God in vain [that is, lightly or frivolously, in false affirmations or profanely]; for the Lord will not hold him guiltless who takes His name in vain." Exodus 20:7

"But the person who does anything [wrong] willfully and openly, whether he is native-born or a stranger, that one reproaches, reviles, and blasphemes the Lord, and that person shall be cut off from among his people [that the atonement made for them may not include him]." Numbers 15:30

I hear people almost on a daily basis swearing by using God or Jesus' name in anger or astonishment. Blasphemy is a common Hollywood film essential.

Cast out Blasphemers

The early assemblies of believers cast blasphemers and heretics out from their midst and delivered them to satan, meaning, they no longer received the care and support of Christian fellowship. This was to prevent their sin from contaminating others and to hopefully have them repent, turn from sin and be welcomed back to God.

"Among them are Hymenaeus and Alexander, whom I have delivered to Satan in order that they may be disciplined [by punishment and learn] not to blaspheme." 1 Timothy 1:20

"[16] But avoid all empty (vain, useless, idle) talk, for it will lead people into more and more ungodliness.

[17] And their teaching [will devour; it] will eat its way like cancer or spread like gangrene. So, it is with Hymenaeus and Philetus." 2 Timothy 2:16-17

The Unforgiveable Sin

The Holy Spirit is God. Mongrel Christians ignore Him or worse, attack people who work with and operate with The Holy Spirit (i.e. Baptist, cessationist, Jehovah Witness, Mormon, Oneness Pentecostal, etc.).

God says blasphemy against the Holy Spirit is an unforgivable sin.

Jesus said, "[28] Truly and solemnly I say to you, all sins will be forgiven the sons of men, and whatever abusive and blasphemous things they utter;

[29] But whoever speaks abusively against or maliciously misrepresents the Holy Spirit can never get forgiveness, but is guilty of and is in the grasp of an everlasting trespass.

[30] For they persisted in saying, He has an unclean spirit." Mark 3:28-30/Matthew 12:31-32/Luke 12:10

God isn't talking about doubt, unbelief or rejection which most in the world, including carnal Christians are guilty of. In the Bible, heretical leaders witnessed miracles, signs and wonders and consistently, publicly, willfully and wickedly labeled the powers of the Holy Spirit and Jesus to be demonic. Such people have hardened their hearts to God and are defiant to repentance of this sin.

"⁴ For it is impossible [to restore and bring again to repentance] those who have been once for all enlightened, who have consciously tasted the heavenly gift and have become sharers of the Holy Spirit,

⁵ And have felt how good the Word of God is and the mighty powers of the age and world to come,

⁶ If they then deviate from the faith and turn away from their allegiance—[it is impossible] to bring them back to repentance, for (because, while, as long as) they nail upon the cross the Son of God afresh [as far as they are concerned] and are holding [Him] up to contempt and shame and public disgrace." Hebrews 6:4-6

Never come against The Holy Spirit or those who operate with Him exercising His power and gifts, doing miracles, signs and wonders.

Ask the Holy Spirit to baptize you, teach you and guide you in life.

More detail on operating in your spiritual senses in spiritual realms can be found in books recommended at the end of this book.

Holy Spirit Baptism

Despite what religious Pentecostals might say, the Holy Spirit (God) baptism is not a requirement to get into Heaven.

Jesus said the Holy Spirit will provide us with many gifts and blessings so it would be wise to accept the Him into your life. He will lead you through spiritual senses to walk in the right direction for your life and destiny with God.

Jesus said, "But the Comforter (Counselor, Helper, Intercessor, Advocate, Strengthener, Standby), the Holy Spirit, Whom the Father will send in My name [in My place, to represent Me and act on My behalf], He will teach you all things. And He will cause you to recall (will remind you of, bring to your remembrance) everything I have told you." John 14:26

Many wrongly believe that they have the Holy Spirit when they accepted Jesus as their Savior or when they were water baptized.

The Holy Spirit was with the disciples when they walked with Him, yet, they were to wait until Pentecost to receive the baptism of the Holy Spirit. If the baptism of the Holy Spirit comes automatically at the same time as water baptism, why did the disciples need to 'get Him again' at Pentecost? Acts 1:5

As you read the Bible and the book of Acts, you'll notice the changes in the disciples after they received the baptism of the Holy Spirit. He gives many gifts that further our spiritual growth process, including prophecy, working of miracles, wisdom, knowledge, tongues, interpretation of tongues, faith, healing, discernment and more. These gifts will manifest.

Holy Spirit Baptism <u>can</u> happen at water baptism as it did with Jesus. The Holy Ghost/Spirit <u>can</u> come upon you <u>with</u> or <u>without</u> the laying on of hands by a believer. Some doctrines will say this is not true, yet it happened to Jesus and to the disciples and others in Acts.

"And there appeared to them tongues resembling fire, which were separated and distributed and which settled on each one of them. And they were all filled (diffused throughout their souls) with the Holy Spirit and began to speak in other (different, foreign) languages (tongues), as the Spirit [a]kept giving them clear and loud expression [in each tongue in appropriate words]." Acts 2:3-4

When I was a pre-teen, in the mid-1960's, the Holy Spirit came upon me when I asked Him to, when I was alone in my room. I'd never heard of such a thing at my religious "church" nor had any books to guide me other than the Bible. It was such an in-filling, that I held onto the side of my bed as I thought I was going to fall out.

The Holy Spirit is God, doesn't abide by humanity's religious restrictions. If there is no one to impart or lay hands on you for this baptism, ask the Holy Spirit to baptize you and come upon you as He did those at Pentecost.

He will.

And ask the Holy Spirit <u>every day</u> to continually fill you and recharge you.

Trust in and love God, not the world.

"Do not love or cherish the world or the things that are in the world. If anyone loves the world, love for the Father is not in him." 1 John 2:15

CHAPTER 25
Prayer

P<small>RAYER IS NOT</small> a requirement to get into Heaven but it's being including in this book as God desires it of us and it's extremely beneficial to us in many ways.

"Do not fret or have any anxiety about anything, but in every circumstance and in everything, by prayer and petition (definite requests), with thanksgiving, continue to make your wants known to God." Philippians 4:6

"Be unceasing in prayer [praying perseveringly]." 1 Thessalonians 5:17

Prayer is your communicating and having a relationship with God. And obtaining peace, comfort, wisdom, His assistance, and His perfect will. God asks us to pray for government, pray for the sick, pray for lost sheep living in sin, and pray for others, so they can get into Heaven.

You can talk to Him about anything and everything. He loves you more so than any person ever could. He desires your connection with Him. Prayer is not some boring, memorized recitation, typical in religious institutions, nor is it a flesh-driven "gimmie list." Speak and then listen to that inner voice.

God can initiate prayer with you perhaps to warn you about something or to bring a sin to your attention that needs dealing with or to advise you on a direction to take in life. Maybe to pray for someone else.

Praying in your spiritual language, referred to usually as "speaking in tongues," can also be done (1 Corinthians 14:2).

More information on that in recommended books or can be found in your Bible or online.

Pray from your heart to Father God (of course you can talk with Jesus and The Holy Spirit too).

Jesus said, "[7] And when you pray, do not heap up phrases (multiply words, repeating the same ones over and over) as the Gentiles do, for they think they will be heard for their much speaking.

[8] Do not be like them, for your Father knows what you need before you ask Him.

[9] Pray, therefore, like this: Our Father Who is in heaven, hallowed (kept holy) be Your name.

¹⁰ Your kingdom come, Your will be done on earth as it is in heaven.

¹¹ Give us this day our daily bread.

¹² And forgive us our debts, as we also have forgiven ([e]left, remitted, and let go of the debts, and have given up resentment against) our debtors.

¹³ And lead (bring) us not into temptation, but deliver us from the evil one. For Yours is the kingdom and the power and the glory forever. Amen." Matthew 6:7-13

HEAVEN'S AXIOMS

1ST AXIOM
Believe and Declare Jesus as Your Lord and Savior

Jesus said we must be born again to enter Heaven.

"Jesus answered him, I assure you, most solemnly I tell you, that unless a person is born again (anew, from above), he cannot ever see (know, be acquainted with, and experience) the kingdom of God." John 3:3

Our earthly mother gave us physical birth. God gives us spiritual birth if we accept it, as we are all born spiritually dead.

"For just as [because of their union of nature] in Adam all people die, so also [by virtue of their union of nature] shall all in Christ be made alive." 1 Corinthians 15:22

Don't confuse this or replace this or blend this, as billions do, with reincarnation (i.e. Buddhism, Hinduism, Jainism, Sikhism) or some kind of enlightenment ritual (i.e. New Age beliefs or yoga meditation) or spiritual energy practices (i.e. demonology, naturism, occult, paganism, psychics, séance, sorcery, wicca, witchcraft, etc.).

God Loves You

"For God so greatly loved and dearly prized the world that He [even] gave up His only begotten (unique) Son, so that whoever believes in (trusts in, clings to, relies on) Him shall not perish (come to destruction, be lost) but have eternal (everlasting) life." John 3:16

"But God shows and clearly proves His [own] love for us by the fact that while we were still sinners, Christ (the Messiah, the Anointed One) died for us." Romans 5:8

"For God so greatly loved and dearly prized the world that He [even] gave up His only begotten (unique) Son, so that whoever believes in (trusts in, clings to, relies on) Him shall not perish (come to destruction, be lost) but have eternal (everlasting) life." John 3:16

"And [besides] we ourselves have seen (have deliberately and steadfastly contemplated) and bear witness that the Father has sent the Son [as the] Savior of the world." 1 John 4:14

"For there [is only] one God, and [only] one Mediator between God and men, the Man Christ Jesus." 1 Timothy 2:5

All May Be Saved

Jesus said, "Behold, I stand at the door and knock; if anyone hears and listens to and heeds My voice and opens the door, I will come in to him and will eat with him, and he [will eat] with Me." Revelation 3:20

"For everyone who calls upon the name of the Lord [invoking Him as Lord] will be saved." Romans 10:13

"Jesus answered him, I assure you, most solemnly I tell you, that unless a person is born again (anew, from above), he cannot ever see (know, be acquainted with, and experience) the kingdom of God. "John 3:3

"And there is salvation in and through no one else, for there is no other name under heaven given among men by and in which we must be saved." Acts 4:12

Assurance as a Believer

"Because if you acknowledge and confess with your lips that Jesus is Lord and, in your heart, believe (adhere to, trust in, and rely on the truth) that God raised Him from the dead, you will be saved." Romans 10:9

"But to as many as did receive and welcome Him, He gave the authority (power, privilege, right) to become the children of God, that is, to those who believe in (adhere to, trust in, and rely on) His name." John 1:12

"But these are written (recorded) in order that you may believe that Jesus is the Christ (the Anointed One), the Son of God, and that through believing and cleaving to and trusting and relying upon Him you may have life through (in) His name [through Who He is]." John 20:31

Whether through blind faith or hearing/reading/scientific/mathematical/researched developed faith or a supernatural road-to-Damascus Acts 9 type faith in Jesus as their Savior, one must take that faith or acceptance of truth and verbally declare that Jesus Christ is their Lord and Savior.

"He who believes [who adheres to and trusts in and relies on the Gospel and Him Whom it sets forth] and is baptized will be saved [from the penalty of eternal death]; but he who does not believe [who does not adhere to and trust in and rely on the Gospel and Him Whom it sets forth] will be condemned." Mark 16:16

"Who is [such a] liar as he who denies that Jesus is the Christ (the Messiah)? He is the antichrist (the antagonist of Christ), who [habitually] denies and refuses to acknowledge the Father and the Son. No one who [habitually] denies (disowns) the Son even has the Father. Whoever confesses (acknowledges and has) the Son has the Father also." 1 John 2:22-23

Acceptance doesn't mean you recite a few words and carry on with your old life. Acceptance means after you verbally confess Him as your Lord and Savior, you will follow God's Word.

Some may think this is a non-issue, yet have you <u>personally</u> accepted Jesus?

A woman that I knew in her sixties, that had been attending "church" since she was a child, <u>had never personally</u> accepted Jesus as her personal Lord and Savior. It seems unusual, but attending a "church" or owning a Bible doesn't mean you're getting into Heaven.

Be sure.

Acknowledge and Receive Him

Jesus said, "Therefore, everyone who acknowledges Me before men and confesses Me [out of a state of oneness with Me], I will also acknowledge him before My Father Who is in heaven and confess [that I am abiding in] him." Matthew 10:32

To make your decision now to receive Jesus Christ as your Lord and Savior, repeat out loud something like this, "Heavenly Father, I am a sinner and I believe that the Lord Jesus Christ died for all my sins on the cross and was raised for my justification; and His blood sacrifice has paid the penalty for all my sins. I do now receive and confess Jesus Christ as my personal Lord and Savior."

After receiving Jesus Christ into your heart, move on to the additional AXIOMs.

Those claiming that this 1st AXIOM is all that's required to get into Heaven, refer to Luke 23:39-43 of the criminal on the cross next to Jesus as an example to justify their position. This man and all before him, were under the Hebrew Old Covenant. The Old Covenant was the Law (hundreds of laws), with a different temple system, a different priest system, a different sacrifice, etc. Jesus' death, resurrection and ascension into Heaven activated the New Covenant.

Those who prefer to gamble with their eternity by ignoring HEAVENs AXIOMs have until their last breath to reconsider their position as there's no reprieve afterwards.

"And just as it is appointed for [all] men once to die, and after that the [certain] judgment." Hebrews 9:27

Praying and holding mass for the dead (Roman Catholicism) and baptism for the dead (Mormonism) is futile. Doing HEAVENs AXIOMs as a proxy for the dead isn't Biblical.

2ND AXIOM
Repent

ONE CAN BELIEVE Jesus is the Savior, but say they're not willing to relinquish sin or repent of sin for themselves yet, as they want to "do it later" or "need to do more research" as justification for keeping their sinful lifestyle.

People will disagree on what is classified as sin. This usually means they want to keep their "pet sins."

Sin will keep you from getting into Heaven.

All Are Sinners

"As it is written, None is righteous, just and truthful and upright and conscientious, no, not one." Romans 3:10

"Since all have sinned and are falling short of the honor and glory which God bestows and receives." Romans 3:23

"For the wages which sin pays is death, but the [bountiful] free gift of God is eternal life through (in union with) Jesus Christ our Lord." Romans 6:23

"Therefore, as sin came into the world through one man, and death as the result of sin, so death spread to all men, [no one being able to stop it or to escape its power] because all men sinned." Romans 5:12

"⁸ If we say we have no sin [refusing to admit that we are sinners], we delude and lead ourselves astray, and the Truth [which the Gospel presents] is not in us [does not dwell in our hearts].

⁹ If we [freely] admit that we have sinned and confess our sins, He is faithful and just (true to His own nature and promises) and will forgive our sins [dismiss our lawlessness] and [continuously] cleanse us from all unrighteousness [everything not in conformity to His will in purpose, thought, and action].

¹⁰ If we say (claim) we have not sinned, we contradict His Word and make Him out to be false and a liar, and His Word is not in us [the divine message of the Gospel is not in our hearts]." 1 John 1:8-10

Repent and Turn from Sin

Sin is rebellion and disobedience to God. We receive forgiveness or pardoning of sin through repentance.

God doesn't say we repent to a priest or leader of some religious system. We repent to God.

"He who covers his transgressions will not prosper, but whoever confesses and forsakes his sins will obtain mercy." Proverbs 28:13

"And saying, Repent (think differently; change your mind, regretting your sins and changing your conduct), for the kingdom of heaven is at hand." Matthew 3:2

Make a deliberate effort to avoid sin and repent to God when you deliberately, ignorantly or mistakenly sin. Repent means that we truly regret and turn away from sin to God.

Don't fall into the trap of believing that you don't sin because you don't do such awful things like murder or commit adultery. God considers the sin of murder and committing adultery when done in thought, not just as an act.

Jesus said, "[21] You have heard that it was said to the men of old, You shall not kill (murder), and whoever kills (murders) shall be liable to and unable to escape the punishment imposed by the court.

²² But I say to you that everyone who continues to be angry with his brother or harbors malice (enmity of heart) against him shall be liable to and unable to escape the punishment imposed by the court; and whoever speaks contemptuously and insultingly to his brother shall be liable to and unable to escape the punishment imposed by the Sanhedrin, and whoever says, You cursed fool! [You empty-headed idiot!] shall be liable to and unable to escape the hell (Gehenna) of fire." Matthew 5:21-22

Notice here Jesus says those who are angry or have hate towards another is considered a murderer and <u>will lose their salvation</u> unless they repent.

Jesus said, "But I say to you that everyone who so much as looks at a woman with evil desire for her has already committed adultery with her in his heart." Matthew 5:28

Don't let any Sin Survive in You

Others don't consider many small things need repentance such as being liars, gossipers, idol worshippers, boasters and deceivers or living by their own set of rules or doctrines, rather than God's. Many believe they are a "good person" and <u>never</u> ask for forgiveness for sin, nor forgive others who offend them. They are therefore living in sin.

Many believe they can do whatever they want; thinking that they will just repent afterwards or confess and say a few prayers and all is well again to continue in their willful sins.

God is not a fool… such <u>thinking</u> leads to spiritual death.

Remember Jesus said, "²¹ Not everyone who says to Me, Lord, Lord, will enter the kingdom of heaven, but he who does the will of My Father Who is in heaven.

"²² Many will say to Me on that day, Lord, Lord, have we not prophesied in Your name and driven out demons in Your name and done many mighty works in Your name?

²³ And then I will say to them openly (publicly), I never knew you; depart from Me, you who act wickedly [disregarding My commands]." Matthew 7:21-23

Again, each person will be judged according to <u>their</u> works.

"¹¹ Then I saw a great white throne and the One Who was seated upon it, from Whose presence and from the sight of Whose face earth and sky fled away, and no place was found for them.

¹² I [also] saw the dead, great and small; they stood before the throne, and books were opened. Then another book was opened, which is [the Book] of Life. And the dead were judged (sentenced) by what they had done [their whole way of feeling and

acting, their aims and endeavors] in accordance with what was recorded in the books.

[13] And the sea delivered up the dead who were in it, death and Hades (the state of death or disembodied existence) surrendered the dead in them, and all were tried and their cases determined by what they had done [according to their motives, aims, and works].

[14] Then death and Hades (the state of death or disembodied existence) were thrown into the lake of fire. This is the second death, the lake of fire.

[15] And if anyone's [name] was not found recorded in the Book of Life, he was hurled into the lake of fire." Revelation 20:11-15

It is each one's responsibility to find out what is acceptable to <u>God</u>, <u>not</u> what is acceptable to their "church" or to a personal ideology. Sincerely ask your Heavenly Father to forgive you of all your sins, which were all paid for by the blood sacrifice of Jesus Christ.

Once a Day

Analyze your life against God's Word on sin and <u>every day,</u> confess and ask for forgiveness. Repent as soon as you sin is best or at least once a day, go to Father for forgiveness of any obvious and hidden sin.

Jesus said, "And said, Truly I say to you, unless you repent (change, turnabout) and become like little children [trusting, lowly, loving, forgiving], you can never enter the kingdom of heaven [at all]." Matthew 18:3

"Remember then from what heights you have fallen. Repent (change the inner man to meet God's will) and do the works you did previously [when first you knew the Lord], or else I will visit you and remove your lampstand from its place, unless you change your mind and repent." Revelation 2:10

"For if we go on deliberately and willingly sinning after once acquiring the knowledge of the Truth, there is no longer any sacrifice left to atone for [our] sins [no further offering to which to look forward]." Hebrews 10:26

We must not seek or decide to sin/deliberately go against or refuse God's commands in the Bible.

Be sorrowful for offending God and for not following His will.

You have no entry into Heaven without true repentance.

Be vigilant in dealing with sin.

Heaven Celebrates Your Entry

"Thus, I tell you, there will be more joy in heaven over one [especially] wicked person who repents (changes his mind, abhorring his errors and misdeeds, and determines to enter upon a better course of life) than over ninety-nine righteous persons who have no need of repentance." Luke 15:7

3ʳᴅ AXIOM
Water Baptism

This is a very controversial topic in religious circles which doesn't need to be if they look to God's Word.

Some will say water baptism isn't a requirement for getting into Heaven and others disagree.

What does God say?

Jesus said, "He who believes [who adheres to and trusts in and relies on the Gospel and Him Whom it sets forth] and is baptized will be saved [from the penalty of eternal death]; but he who does not believe [who does not adhere to and trust in and rely on the Gospel and Him Whom it sets forth] will be condemned." Mark 16:16

Jesus said, "Go then and make disciples of all the nations, baptizing them into the name of the Father and of the Son and of the Holy Spirit." Matthew 28:19

"And he ordered that they be baptized in the name of Jesus Christ (the Messiah)." Acts 10:48a

"And baptism, which is a figure [of their deliverance], does now also save you [from inward questionings and fears], not by the removing of outward body filth [bathing], but by [providing you with] the answer of a good and clear conscience (inward cleanness and peace) before God [because you are demonstrating what you believe to be yours] through the resurrection of Jesus Christ." 1 Peter 3:21

"[There is] one Lord, one faith, one baptism." Ephesians 4:5

"[3] Are you ignorant of the fact that all of us who have been baptized into Christ Jesus were baptized into His death?

[4] We were buried therefore with Him by the baptism into death, so that just as Christ was raised from the dead by the glorious [power] of the Father, so we too might [habitually] live and behave in newness of life." Romans 6:3-4

"[26] For in Christ Jesus you are all sons of God through faith.

[27] For as many [of you] as were baptized into Christ [into a spiritual union and communion with Christ, the Anointed One, the Messiah] have put on (clothed yourselves with) Christ." Galatians 3:26-27

Water baptism is a spiritual act, identifying with Christ's death, burial and resurrection, signifying your new spiritual birth as a new follower of Christ. A person has life in the womb, but has not been born. Think of it like a person existing in the embryonic fluid or water in the womb, coming forth or being born into a new spiritual life. We bury our old self and are born into life as a new creature (2 Corinthians 5:17).

"Therefore, if any person is [ingrafted] in Christ (the Messiah) he is a new creation (a new creature altogether); the old [previous moral and spiritual condition] has passed away. Behold, the fresh and new has come!" 2 Corinthians 5:17

What is a Water Baptism?

Disagreements exist on what qualifies as water baptism.

Some say it's alright if an infant is water baptized; others accept sprinkling with water, rather than full immersion; others will say only their "church" baptism is acceptable and some insist you must take up to a yearlong course before you can be water baptized.

The theories and doctrines are plentiful.

Ordained Baptism?

Is a special "ordained" priest or pastor required for a water baptism to be "official."

No.

Any believer can baptize you, as John the Baptist was not a seminary or Bible College graduate, neither was Jesus nor any of the disciples.

If you accept Jesus and repent yet are alone or surrounded by infidels and heretics, water baptize yourself (such as if death is imminent in a war zone).

Full Immersion or Sprinkling?

Looking to the Word of God, we see that Jesus, who did nothing of His own, but what His Father in Heaven had Him do, had a full, water-immersion baptism, as an adult.

Biblically, a full-immersion baptism is how our Father led Jesus.

Typical practice in the Bible was, adults received a water baptism after acceptance of Jesus as their Lord and Savior and after repentance of sin.

Further detailed information on water baptism is available from *"The Didache,"* in that the disciples of Jesus did full immersion in running water and if that wasn't available, then in standing water, then down to pouring water on the head if the other ways weren't available.

Infant Baptism?

Some will argue that although the Bible doesn't specifically mention infant baptism, entire households were water baptized which must have included infants.

Water baptism was normally done after a person did the first two HEAVENs AXIOMs…

"And Peter answered them, Repent (change your views and purpose to accept the will of God in your inner selves instead of rejecting it) and be baptized, every one of you, in the name of Jesus Christ for the forgiveness of and release from your sins; and you shall receive the gift of the Holy Spirit." Acts 2:38

"But when they believed the good news (the Gospel) about the kingdom of God and the name of Jesus Christ (the Messiah) as Philip preached it, they were baptized, both men and women." Acts 8:12

An infant would be unable to declare acceptance of Jesus as their Savior and unable to repent. However, the early gatherings of believers did baptize those too young to speak for themselves.

If you were dedicated to God and baptized/sprinkled with water as an infant, as I was, I would recommend that you go somewhere and receive a <u>full immersion</u> water baptism. I did so in the Jordan River in Israel decades ago.

Repeat Baptism?

Some assemblies require a person to be rebaptized into their "church" as any others don't count. This is a man-made doctrine.

Take a Course?

Some assemblies require a person to take a course or confirmation classes before a person can be baptized. This is a man-made doctrine.

Baptism of Dead?

Standing in as a proxy to perform water baptism (Mormonism) for the dead is a man-mad doctrine.

Get some Water

Don't fight God. After you have accepted Jesus as your Lord and Savior and repented, be baptized in water.

An example of a water baptism: Being totally immersed 3 times under the water while another person says something like, "I baptize you in the name of the Father and the Son and the Holy Spirit," as you come up out of the water and down again 3 times. Accept this as a supernatural act of joining with Jesus' resurrection into a new life.

If full immersion isn't available or possible, such as a person on their death-bed, use a bottle of water.

4ᵀᴴ AXIOM
Forgive Others the Sins they've Committed against You

Covered at length in Chapter 23.

Jesus said, "For if you forgive people their trespasses [their reckless and willful sins, leaving them, letting them go, and giving up resentment], your heavenly Father will also forgive you. But if you do not forgive others their trespasses [their reckless and willful sins, leaving them, letting them go, and giving up resentment], neither will your Father forgive you your trespasses." Matthew 6:14-15

"So also, my heavenly Father will deal with every one of you if you do not freely forgive your brother from your heart his offenses. Matthew 18:35 See also Mark 11:25-26

If you don't forgive others, God <u>will not</u> forgive you.

5ᵀᴴ AXIOM
Cease Heresy

Stay Sanctified

R‌EFER TO PREVIOUS material, especially Chapter 19.

Don't add false doctrines, compromise with or cherry-pick with the Bible. Ignoring parts of God's Word is also heresy. Avoid those who are cursed.

"If anyone comes to you and does not bring this doctrine [is disloyal to what Jesus Christ taught], do not receive him [do not accept him, do not welcome or admit him] into [your] house or bid him Godspeed or give him any encouragement." 2 John 1:10

"But now I write to you not to associate with anyone who bears the name of [Christian] brother if he is known to be guilty of immorality or greed, or is an idolater [whose soul is devoted to any object that usurps the place of God], or is a person with a foul tongue [railing, abusing, reviling, slandering], or is a drunkard or a swindler or a robber. [No] you must not so much as eat with such a person." 1 Corinthians 5:11

"¹⁷ I appeal to you, brethren, to be on your guard concerning those who create dissensions and difficulties and cause divisions, in opposition to the doctrine (the teaching) which you have been taught. [I warn you to turn aside from them, to] avoid them.

¹⁸ For such persons do not serve our Lord Christ but their own appetites and base desires, and by ingratiating and flattering speech, they beguile the hearts of the unsuspecting and simpleminded [people]." Romans 16:17-18

"¹⁶ But avoid all empty (vain, useless, idle) talk, for it will lead people into more and more ungodliness.

¹⁷ And their teaching [will devour; it] will eat its way like cancer or spread like gangrene. So it is with Hymenaeus and Philetus." 2 Timothy 2:16-17 see 1 Timothy 1:20

Don't let Heresy rob you of Your Inheritance

"²¹ Because when they knew and recognized Him as God, they did not honor and glorify Him as God or give Him thanks. But instead they became futile and godless in their thinking [with vain imaginings, foolish reasoning, and stupid speculations] and their senseless minds were darkened.

²² Claiming to be wise, they became fools [professing to be smart, they made simpletons of themselves].

²³ And by them the glory and majesty and excellence of the immortal God were exchanged for and represented by images, resembling mortal man and birds and beasts and reptiles.

²⁴ Therefore God gave them up in the lusts of their [own] hearts to sexual impurity, to the dishonoring of their bodies among themselves [abandoning them to the degrading power of sin],

²⁵ Because they exchanged the truth of God for a lie and worshiped and served the creature rather than the Creator, Who is blessed forever! Amen (so be it).

²⁶ For this reason God gave them over and abandoned them to vile affections and degrading passions. For their women exchanged their natural function for an unnatural and abnormal one,

²⁷ And the men also turned from natural relations with women and were set ablaze (burning out, consumed) with lust for one another—men committing shameful acts with men and suffering in their own bodies and personalities the inevitable consequences and penalty of their wrong-doing and going astray, which was [their] fitting retribution.

²⁸ And so, since they did not see fit to acknowledge God or approve of Him or consider Him worth the knowing, God gave

them over to a base and condemned mind to do things not proper or decent but loathsome,

²⁹ Until they were filled (permeated and saturated) with every kind of unrighteousness, iniquity, grasping and covetous greed, and malice. [They were] full of envy and jealousy, murder, strife, deceit and treachery, ill will and cruel ways. [They were] secret backbiters and gossipers,

³⁰ Slanderers, hateful to and hating God, full of insolence, arrogance, [and] boasting; inventors of new forms of evil, disobedient and undutiful to parents.

³¹ [They were] without understanding, conscienceless and faithless, heartless and loveless [and] merciless.

³² Though they are fully aware of God's righteous decree that those who do such things deserve to die, they not only do them themselves but approve and applaud others who practice them." Romans 1:21-32 (see also Leviticus 18:22 and also 1 Corinthians 6:9-10)

Study 2 Peter 2 and Galatians 1:8-9 again.

6ᵀᴴ AXIOM
Cease Blasphemy

Jesus said, "²⁸Truly and solemnly I say to you, all sins will be forgiven the sons of men, and whatever abusive and blasphemous things they utter;

²⁹But whoever speaks abusively against or maliciously misrepresents the Holy Spirit can never get forgiveness, but is guilty of and is in the grasp of an everlasting trespass." Mark 3:28-29

"Among them are Hymenaeus and Alexander, whom I have delivered to Satan in order that they may be disciplined [by punishment and learn] not to blaspheme." 1 Timothy 1:20

Refer to Chapter 24.

7ᵀᴴ AXIOM
Be Faithful Until Death

D ON'T LOSE WHAT you gained.

"⁴ For it is impossible [to restore and bring again to repentance] those who have been once for all enlightened, who have consciously tasted the heavenly gift and have become sharers of the Holy Spirit,

⁵ And have felt how good the Word of God is and the mighty powers of the age and world to come,

⁶ If they then deviate from the faith and turn away from their allegiance—[it is impossible] to bring them back to repentance, for (because, while, as long as) they nail upon the cross the Son of God afresh [as far as they are concerned] and are holding [Him] up to contempt and shame and public disgrace." Hebrews 6:4-6

"For if we go on deliberately and willingly sinning after once acquiring the knowledge of the Truth, there is no longer any sacrifice left to atone for [our] sins [no further offering to which to look forward]." Hebrews 10:26

"Anyone who runs on ahead [of God] and does not abide in the doctrine of Christ [who is not content with what He taught] does not have God; but he who continues to live in the doctrine (teaching) of Christ [does have God], he has both the Father and the Son." 2 John 9

"Let me warn you therefore, beloved, that knowing these things beforehand, you should be on your guard, lest you be carried away by the error of lawless and wicked [persons and] fall from your own [present] firm condition [your own steadfastness of mind]." 2 Peter 3:17

"Look to yourselves (take care) that you may not lose (throw away or destroy) all that we and you have labored for, but that you may [persevere until you] win and receive back a perfect reward [in full]." 2 John 8

Jesus said, "If you [really] love Me, you will keep (obey) My commands." John 14:15

Faithful means obedience every day to following God's Word to the end of your earthly life.

"24 Do you not know that in a race all the runners compete, but [only] one receives the prize? So run [your race] that you may lay hold [of the prize] and make it yours.

²⁵ Now every athlete who goes into training conducts himself temperately and restricts himself in all things. They do it to win a wreath that will soon wither, but we [do it to receive a crown of eternal blessedness] that cannot wither.

²⁶ Therefore I do not run uncertainly (without definite aim). I do not box like one beating the air and striking without an adversary.

²⁷ But [like a boxer] I buffet my body [handle it roughly, discipline it by hardships] and subdue it, for fear that after proclaiming to others the Gospel and things pertaining to it, I myself should become unfit [not stand the test, be unapproved and rejected as a counterfeit]." 1 Corinthians 9:24-27

"Thus says the Lord of hosts: If you will walk in My ways and keep My charge, then also you shall rule My house and have charge of My courts, and I will give you access [to My presence] and places to walk among these who stand here." Zecheriah 3:7

Jesus said, "I assure you, most solemnly I tell you, the person whose ears are open to My words [who listens to My message] and believes and trusts in and clings to and relies on Him Who sent Me has (possesses now) eternal life. And he does not come into judgment [does not incur sentence of judgment, will not come under condemnation], but he has already passed over out of death into life." John 5:24

"And from the days of John the Baptist until the present time, the kingdom of heaven has endured violent assault, and violent men seize it by force [as a precious prize—a share in the heavenly kingdom is sought with most ardent zeal and intense exertion]." Matthew 11:12

Don't ever Stop

"Be faithful until death, and I will give you the crown of life." Revelation 2:10 NKJV

Beyond Getting Into Heaven

God Anointing

"²¹Now he who establishes us with you in Christ and has anointed us is God,

²² who also has sealed us and given us the Spirit in our hearts as a guarantee." 2 Corinthians 1:21-22 NKJV

Jesus said in a parable in Matthew 20:1-16 that everyone receives a full inheritance in Heaven no matter when in their lives that they accept Him.

Treasures in Heaven

Jesus said, "¹⁹ Do not gather and heap up and store up for yourselves treasures on earth, where moth and rust and worm consume and destroy, and where thieves break through and steal.

[20] But gather and heap up and store for yourselves treasures in heaven, where neither moth nor rust nor worm consume and destroy, and where thieves do not break through and steal;

[21] For where your treasure is, there will your heart be also." Matthew 6:19-21

Jesus states that we receive a full inheritance of everything that Heaven has to offer, which will lack nothing.

We receive eternal citizenship in Heaven, numerous titles, crowns, love, joy, peace and other rewards covered in Chapter 11.

What other treasures would God and Heaven consider to be treasures that we should gather, heap and store?

God treasures us, you and me and everyone He created. He wants each of us enjoy eternity with Him. That is His treasure.

Also, all those we helped reach Heaven we would consider, along with God, to be great treasures.

We can gather, heap and store up treasures in Heaven by following Jesus' commands to go, make disciples, baptize and teach, which is called The Great Commission.

"[18] And Jesus came and spoke to them, saying, "All authority has been given to Me in heaven and on earth.

¹⁹ Go therefore and make disciples of all the nations, baptizing them in the name of the Father and of the Son and of the Holy Spirit,

²⁰ teaching them to observe all things that I have commanded you; and lo, I am with you always, even to the end of the age." Amen." Matthew 28:18-20 NKJV also Mark 16:14-18; Luke 24:44-49; John 20:21

But, what can I do?

Many will say that they're not evangelists or teachers so how can they build up these treasures.

There are many ways to participate such as:

1. Passing this book along to a child, adult or even go through it with someone on their death bed.

2. Mail this book anonymously to family and/or friends.

3. Mail this book to leaders and influencers who are on the wrong path. Their shifting directions can multiply your action out to many others that they impact.

   An old carpenter, Christian Wolfkes, in an obscure Romanian village, taught a visiting Jew about Christ in the late 1930's. This former Jew, Richard Wurmbrand, became an internationally known leader whose books have reached millions even to this day. That old carpenter's one action certainly produced storehouses of treasures in Heaven.

4. You can donate time and/or money to support The Great Commission being undertaken directly by others.

   Be careful in doing this as you don't want to invest in the wrong gardens that produce dead fruit for you and any others.

5. Pray and intercede for others.

"The earnest prayer of a righteous person has great power and produces wonderful results." James 5:16b NLT

My sweet, loving, humble aunt, prayed and interceded for many others for decades, into her late 80's.

"[36] When He (Jesus) saw the throngs, He was moved with pity and sympathy for them, because they were bewildered (harassed and distressed and dejected and helpless), like sheep without a shepherd.

[37] Then He said to His disciples, The harvest is indeed plentiful, but the laborers are few.

[38] So pray to the Lord of the harvest to force out and thrust laborers into His harvest." Matthew 9:36-38

Heaven's Treasure Map to The Meaning of Life

JESUS SAID, "I assure you and most solemnly say to you, anyone who believes in Me [as Savior] will also do the things that I do; and he will do even greater things than these [in extent and outreach], because I am going to the Father." John 14:12 AMP

How can we do greater works than Jesus did is a common question?

Especially when we read this next scripture verse.

"And there are also many other things which Jesus did. If they should be all recorded one by one [in detail], I suppose that even the world itself could not contain (have room for) the books that would be written." John 21:25

We follow Heaven's Treasure Map that He gave us to accomplish it, that's how.

When we read the Bible, we're given a Treasure Map of how to prepare, start and run our lives... building treasures in Heaven... The Great Commission.

Jesus was fully immersed water baptized as an adult (Matthew 3:13; Mark 1:9; Luke 3:21; John 1:33), received the Holy Spirit baptism/power (Matthew 3:16; Mark 1:10; Luke 3:22; John 1:32), went through wilderness time (Matthew 4:1; Mark 1:12; Luke 4:1), fasted forty days (Matthew 4:2; Luke 4:2), overcame temptation (Matthew 4:3-11; Mark 1:14; Luke 4:2-13), then started preaching repentance followed by demonstrations of God's power (miracles, signs and wonders), and God's Standards, expectations and truth of how to be reconciled with Him... the Gospel.

Remember that Jesus, the disciples and Paul and each of us are the temples of God, allowing the Holy Spirit to operate through them and us with power, "Now to Him Who, by (in consequence of) the [action of His] power that is at work within us, is able to [carry out His purpose and] do superabundantly, far over and above all that we [dare] ask or think [infinitely beyond our highest prayers, desires, thoughts, hopes, or dreams]. Ephesians 3:20

God's Will be done, Not Yours

Another key takeaway is Jesus never did His own will, "For I have come down from heaven not to do My own will and purpose but to do the will and purpose of Him Who sent Me." John 6:38

And, "So Jesus answered them by saying, I assure you, most solemnly I tell you, the Son is able to do nothing of Himself (of His own accord); but He is able to do only what He sees the Father doing, for whatever the Father does is what the Son does in the same way [in His turn]." John 5:19

And, "I am able to do nothing from Myself [independently, of My own accord—but only as I am taught by God and as I get His orders]. Even as I hear, I judge [I decide as I am bidden to decide. As the voice comes to Me, so I give a decision], and My judgment is right (just, righteous), because I do not seek or consult My own will [I have no desire to do what is pleasing to Myself, My own aim, My own purpose] but only the will and pleasure of the Father Who sent Me." John 5:30

Multiplication

Part of Heaven's Treasure Map is that Jesus gathered up twelve to learn from Him (Luke 6:13) and appointed at least another 70 (Luke 10:1), totaling 82.

Thousands of others of course heard and observed Him.

He taught them for 3 and a half years about the Kingdom of God, their place in it, God's truth, righteousness, healing, deliverance, wisdom, knowledge, working with the Holy Spirit, how to conduct their own lives, and to develop others (disciples). He taught the importance and duty of multiplication.

Looking at Jesus' initial 12 disciples, if 12 grew out from each and they all did the same and so on as directed, we'd have...

JESUS
12X12=144
144X12=1728
1728X12=20736
20736X12=248,832
248,832X12=2,985,984
2,985,984X12=35,831,808
35,831,808X12=429,981,696
429,981,696X12=5,159,780,352

... over 5 BILLION treasures getting into Heaven rather quickly.

Much faster if you went with 82-fold, as Jesus did.

What Happened?

How many do you know who are following Heaven's Treasure Map given to us on how to run their lives let alone producing at least 12 people getting into Heaven and so on?

We discussed how priests, pastors, leaders, seminaries, Bible colleges and universities, are supposed to follow The Map aren't, let alone individuals.

Thus, instead of billions living in eternal bliss, we're at the 95%+ in rudderless lives who aren't getting into Heaven.

These "experts" stand in front of people, using "wise and persuasive words" (1 Corinthians 2:4), gathering offerings, singing a few songs and then do it all again next week. This isn't in The Map.

A few do mentor or write spiritually inspired teaching books, do USB's, YouTube videos, social media, etc., in hopes that people will learn and reproduce. These are all very productive means of obtaining widespread results.

I praise those who do offer sound teachings and testimonies as it saves those from struggling unnecessarily over rough territory.

Writing is a great multiplication method, as we know the Word of God has brought many to Christ without them receiving mentoring assistance. Mentoring is more closely following Jesus' example though, as this provides an encouraging role model.

Many Christians read, listen, watch, attend conferences and seminars, but sadly most say, "That was great," but never apply the teachings, never teach others what they've learned, never follow The Map.

Even from the beginning, HEAVEN'S AXIOMS and Heaven's Treasure Map petered out or was being watered down by false gospels, mongrel religions and worldly values as we see from Paul's writings to wayward believers, despite his time spent with them. Christian history up to the 21st Century tells the same story, dead "churches", wallowing in deliberate sin, self-idolizing and compromising with God's Standards.

The Missing Piece

Besides all we've covered, the piece from Heaven's Treasure Map, that "churches" and religious leaders ignore which brings about their failure and the failure of populating Heaven, is that Jesus, the disciples and Paul…

1. Preached about Heaven and then
2. Backed up God's Word with demonstrations of power

"And Jesus went about all the cities and villages, teaching in their synagogues and proclaiming the good news (the Gospel) of the kingdom and curing all kinds of disease and every weakness and infirmity." Matthew 9:35

"And they went out and preached everywhere, while the Lord kept working with them and confirming the message by the attesting signs and miracles that closely accompanied [it]. Amen (so be it)." Mark 16:20

"⁴And my language and my message were not set forth in persuasive (enticing and plausible) words of wisdom, but they were in demonstration of the [Holy] Spirit and power [a proof by the Spirit and power of God, operating on me and stirring in the minds of my hearers the most holy emotions and thus persuading them].

⁵So that your faith might not rest in the wisdom of men (human philosophy), but in the power of God." 1 Corinthians 2:4-5

Demonstration of God's Power Testimony

A blood-thirsty Jewish pharisee named Saul who hunted down Christians couldn't be reached with God's truth except through having God's power directly touch him. Just hearing about and seeing miracles, signs and wonders only deepened his murderous hatred.

After He saw the light as they say (Acts 9), he then used his Roman name, Paul, as he travelled the Mediterranean region to treasure hunt for Heaven. During those years he wrote most of the books of the Bible that still reach and teach people today.

His work continues pouring treasures into Heaven.

We should have a mentor that can trace their lineage back to Jesus, who works in miracles, signs and wonders. Instead, I spent many years sitting around in the pew of a "hymn-sandwich church," thinking I was doing what God wanted. I wasn't taught anything different.

On my own I had to struggle along through a few old books and trial and error to finally and fortunately find God's truth.

Most never get there and so they drift along deaf, dumb and blind to the spiritual realm all their lives, thanks to those who don't handle their responsibilities properly. Religious leaders certainly don't and won't multiply themselves, as that would produce competition that would cut into their profit margin.

Your Turn

Are you producing at least 12 to follow Heaven's Treasure Map?

You don't have to do them all at once… if you woke up just one deceived infidel or one mongrelized heretic or one dormant "pew sitter" a year and mentored them, you'd meet the goal in 12 years.

These 12 then train to do their part to develop themselves and follow the multiplication path.

I don't plan on standing in front of the Judgement Seat one day to explain why I didn't follow God's will on how to operate and live as a believer (Hebrews 9:27).

We don't have to walk through life with 12 people in tow wherever we go. For most of us this wouldn't be practical with jobs and families. You can do this online if in-person mentoring isn't feasible. Or, as I said, pass out this book. Needing a diploma to work with God is a man-made doctrine not a Biblical one. God anoints and appoints and sends out. Surrender to Him.

Encourage people to grow and step away from the pews (and spiritually dead "churches"/leaders) ... to step into their destiny. Train them, mentor them and set them lose to build treasures in Heaven. This may seem to be a difficult task, but with God nothing is impossible. Ask the Holy Spirit how to accomplish this in your life and for the lives of others.

You will never be alone; God will always be with you as He wants you to succeed.

"[24] Then Jesus said to His disciples, "If anyone desires to come after Me, let him deny himself, and take up his cross, and follow Me.

²⁵ For whoever desires to save his life will lose it, but whoever loses his life for My sake will find it.

²⁶ For what profit is it to a man if he gains the whole world, and loses his own soul? Or what will a man give in exchange for his soul?

²⁷ For the Son of Man will come in the glory of His Father with His angels, and then He will reward each according to his works." Matthew 16:24-27 NKJV

Make sure that you're mentoring properly, as I've seen many who operate in miracles, signs and wonders end up on a dark path. They become heretical, leading the trusting and naïve into the lake of fire with them.

You're not responsible for those who ignore your guidance to follow their own mongrel religion.

Also, don't drift off Heaven's Treasure Map to become one of those "advanced" leaders who claim they have deep, insights from God. If you contradict God's Word, even just a portion of it (Galatians 5:9; 1 Corinthians 5:6), you've become one of the blind leading the blind.

Jesus said "Follow Me" to His disciples.

That's you.

Be bold... You're more than a conqueror... Live your life as a Treasure Hunter.

"But in your hearts set Christ apart as holy [and acknowledge Him] as Lord. Always be ready to give a logical defense to anyone who asks you to account for the hope that is in you, but do it courteously and respectfully." 1 Peter 3:15

Afterword

Be Sure You're Getting Into Heaven

MAKING SURE YOU get into Heaven is a priority. Spending and investing your life into the world and its attractions will not serve you well, according to God.

"¹⁵ Do not love or cherish the world or the things that are in the world. If anyone loves the world, love for the Father is not in him.

¹⁶ For all that is in the world—the lust of the flesh [craving for sensual gratification] and the lust of the eyes [greedy longings of the mind] and the pride of life [assurance in one's own resources or in the stability of earthly things]—these do not come from the Father but are from the world [itself].

¹⁷ And the world passes away and disappears, and with it the forbidden cravings (the passionate desires, the lust) of it; but he who does the will of God and carries out His purposes in his life abides (remains) forever." 1 John 2:15-17

All of your work on earth will be examined. You want to stand boldly in front of all your treasures that you built up in Heaven.

"[11] For no other foundation can anyone lay than that which is [already] laid, which is Jesus Christ (the Messiah, the Anointed One).

[12] But if anyone builds upon the Foundation, whether it be with gold, silver, precious stones, wood, hay, straw,

[13] The work of each [one] will become [plainly, openly] known (shown for what it is); for the day [of Christ] will disclose and declare it, because it will be revealed with fire, and the fire will test and critically appraise the character and worth of the work each person has done.

[14] If the work which any person has built on this Foundation [any product of his efforts whatever] survives [this test], he will get his reward.

[15] But if any person's work is burned up [under the test], he will suffer the loss [of it all, losing his reward], though he himself will be saved, but only as [one who has passed] through fire." 1 Corinthians 3:11-15

Enjoy your walk with God all the way into eternity in Heaven as a saint, royal priest, king, lord and joint-heir with God.

AFTERWORD

"¹ Blessed (happy, fortunate, prosperous, and enviable) is the man who walks and lives not in the counsel of the ungodly [following their advice, their plans and purposes], nor stands [submissive and inactive] in the path where sinners walk, nor sits down [to relax and rest] where the scornful [and the mockers] gather.

² But his delight and desire are in the law of the Lord, and on His law (the precepts, the instructions, the teachings of God) he habitually meditates (ponders and studies) by day and by night.

³ And he shall be like a tree firmly planted [and tended] by the streams of water, ready to bring forth its fruit in its season; its leaf also shall not fade or wither; and everything he does shall prosper [and come to maturity].

⁴ Not so the wicked [those disobedient and living without God are not so]. But they are like the chaff [worthless, dead, without substance] which the wind drives away.

⁵ Therefore the wicked [those disobedient and living without God] shall not stand [justified] in the judgment, nor sinners in the congregation of the righteous [those who are upright and in right standing with God].

⁶ For the Lord knows and is fully acquainted with the way of the righteous, but the way of the ungodly [those living outside God's will] shall perish (end in ruin and come to nought)." Psalm 1

"[Born anew] into an inheritance which is beyond the reach of change and decay [imperishable], unsullied and unfading, reserved in heaven for you," 1 Peter 1:4

"Then I heard further [perceiving the distinct words of] a voice from heaven, saying, write this: Blessed (happy, to be envied) are the dead from now on who die in the Lord! Yes, blessed (happy, to be envied indeed), says the Spirit, [in] that they may rest from their labors, for their works (deeds) do follow (attend, accompany) them!" Revelation 14:13

"He went once for all into the [Holy of] Holies [of heaven], not by virtue of the blood of goats and calves [by which to make reconciliation between God and man], but His own blood, having found and secured a complete redemption (an everlasting release for us)." Hebrews 9:12

"And [how you] look forward to and await the coming of His Son from heaven, Whom He raised from the dead—Jesus, Who personally rescues and delivers us out of and from the wrath [bringing punishment] which is coming [upon the impenitent] and draws us to Himself [investing us with all the privileges and rewards of the new life in Christ, the Messiah]." 1 Thessalonians 1:10

[23] Jesus answered, If a person [really] loves Me, he will keep My word [obey My teaching]; and My Father will love him, and We will come to him and make Our home (abode, special dwelling place) with him.

24 Anyone who does not [really] love Me does not observe and obey My teaching. And the teaching which you hear and heed is not Mine, but [comes] from the Father Who sent Me." John 14:23-24

A Mystery

"⁵¹ Take notice! I tell you a mystery (a secret truth, an event decreed by the hidden purpose or counsel of God). We shall not all fall asleep [in death], but we shall all be changed (transformed)

⁵² In a moment, in the twinkling of an eye, at the [sound of the] last trumpet call. For a trumpet will sound, and the dead [in Christ] will be raised imperishable (free and immune from decay), and we shall be changed (transformed).

⁵³ For this perishable [part of us] must put on the imperishable [nature], and this mortal [part of us, this nature that is capable of dying] must put on immortality (freedom from death).

⁵⁴ And when this perishable puts on the imperishable and this that was capable of dying puts on freedom from death, then shall be fulfilled the Scripture that says, Death is swallowed up (utterly vanquished forever) in and unto victory.

⁵⁵ O death, where is your victory? O death, where is your sting?

⁵⁶ Now sin is the sting of death, and sin exercises its power [upon the soul] through [the abuse of] the Law.

⁵⁷ But thanks be to God, Who gives us the victory [making us conquerors] through our Lord Jesus Christ.

⁵⁸ Therefore, my beloved brethren, be firm (steadfast), immovable, always abounding in the work of the Lord [always being superior, excelling, doing more than enough in the service of the Lord], knowing and being continually aware that your labor in the Lord is not futile [it is never wasted or to no purpose]." 1 Corinthians 15:51-58

Through the Eternities of the Eternities

"¹ THEN HE showed me the river whose waters give life, sparkling like crystal, flowing out from the throne of God and of the Lamb

² Through the middle of the broadway of the city; also, on either side of the river was the tree of life with its twelve varieties of fruit, yielding each month its fresh crop; and the leaves of the tree were for the healing and the restoration of the nations.

³ There shall no longer exist there anything that is accursed (detestable, foul, offensive, impure, hateful, or horrible). But the throne of God and of the Lamb shall be in it, and His servants shall worship Him [pay divine honors to Him and do Him holy service].

⁴ They shall see His face, and His name shall be on their foreheads.

⁵ And there shall be no more night; they have no need for lamplight or sunlight, for the Lord God will illuminate them and be their light, and they shall <u>reign [as kings] forever and ever (through the eternities of the eternities)</u>.

⁶ And he [of the seven angels further] said to me, These statements are reliable (worthy of confidence) and genuine (true). And the Lord, the God of the spirits of the prophets, has sent His messenger (angel) to make known and exhibit to His servants what must soon come to pass.

⁷ And behold, I am coming speedily. Blessed (happy and to be envied) is he who observes and lays to heart and keeps the truths of the prophecy (the predictions, consolations, and warnings) contained in this [little] book.

⁸ And I, John, am he who heard and witnessed these things. And when I heard and saw them, I fell prostrate before the feet of the messenger (angel) who showed them to me, to worship him.

⁹ But he said to me, Refrain! [You must not do that!] I am [only] a fellow servant along with yourself and with your brethren the prophets and with those who are mindful of and practice [the truths contained in] the messages of this book. Worship God!

¹⁰ And he [further] told me, Do not seal up the words of the prophecy of this book and make no secret of them, for the time when things are brought to a crisis and the period of their fulfillment is near.

¹¹ He who is unrighteous (unjust, wicked), let him be unrighteous still; and he who is filthy (vile, impure), let him be filthy still; and he who is righteous (just, upright, in right standing with God), let him do right still; and he who is holy, let him be holy still.

¹² Behold, I am coming soon, and I shall bring My wages and rewards with Me, to repay and render to each one just what his own actions and his own work merit.

¹³ I am the Alpha and the Omega, the First and the Last (the Before all and the End of all).

¹⁴ Blessed (happy and to be envied) are those who cleanse their garments, that they may have the authority and right to [approach] the tree of life and to enter through the gates into the city.

¹⁵ [But] without are the dogs and those who practice sorceries (magic arts) and impurity [the lewd, adulterers] and the murderers and idolaters and everyone who loves and deals in falsehood (untruth, error, deception, cheating).

¹⁶ I, Jesus, have sent My messenger (angel) to you to witness and to give you assurance of these things for the churches (assemblies). I am the Root (the Source) and the Offspring of David, the radiant and brilliant Morning Star.

¹⁷ The [Holy] Spirit and the bride (the church, the true Christians) say, Come! And let him who is listening say, Come! And let everyone come who is thirsty [who is painfully conscious of his need of those things by which the soul is refreshed, supported, and strengthened]; and whoever [earnestly] desires to do it, let him come, take, appropriate, and drink the water of Life without cost.

¹⁸ I [personally solemnly] warn everyone who listens to the statements of the prophecy [the predictions and the consolations and admonitions pertaining to them] in this book: If anyone shall add anything to them, God will add and lay upon him the plagues (the afflictions and the calamities) that are recorded and described in this book.

¹⁹ And if anyone cancels or takes away from the statements of the book of this prophecy [these predictions relating to Christ's kingdom and its speedy triumph, together with the consolations and admonitions or warnings pertaining to them], God will cancel and take away from him his share in the tree of life and in the city of holiness (purity and hallowedness), which are described and promised in this book.

²⁰ He Who gives this warning and affirms and testifies to these things says, Yes (it is true). [Surely] I am coming quickly (swiftly, speedily). Amen (so let it be)! Yes, come, Lord Jesus!

²¹ The grace (blessing and favor) of the Lord Jesus Christ (the Messiah) be with all the saints (God's holy people, those set

apart for God, to be, as it were, exclusively His). Amen (so let it be)!" Revelation 22

The True Meaning of Life

THE TRUE MEANING OF LIFE is to reign with God through the eternities of the eternities in Heaven.

"Thus says the Lord of hosts: If you will walk in My ways and keep My charge, then also you shall rule My house and have charge of My courts, and I will give you access [to My presence] and places to walk among these who stand here." Zecheriah 3:7

"16 The Spirit Himself [thus] testifies together with our own spirit, [assuring us] that we are children of God.

17 And if we are [His] children, then we are [His] heirs also: heirs of God and fellow heirs with Christ [sharing His inheritance with Him]; only we must share His suffering if we are to share His glory." Romans 6:16-17

"Therefore, you are no longer a slave (bond servant) but a son; and if a son, then [it follows that you are] an heir by the aid of God, through Christ." Galatians 4:7

"And He raised us up together with Him and made us sit down together [giving us joint seating with Him] in the heavenly sphere [by virtue of our being] in Christ Jesus (the Messiah, the Anointed One)." Ephesians 2:6

"If we endure, we shall also reign with Him. If we deny and disown and reject Him, He will also deny and disown and reject us." 2 Timothy 2:12

"He who overcomes (is victorious), I will grant him to sit beside Me on My throne, as I Myself overcame (was victorious) and sat down beside My Father on His throne." Revelation 3:21

Supplemental Material

Budge, W., (1907), *Paradise of the Desert Fathers*, Volume 1 & 2, Chatto & Windus.

Collins, A., (2018), *The Silver Bullet of God: A Field Manual for Superheroes*, Crown of Life Ministries.

Collins, A., (2018), *The Way: Visit Heaven Whenever You Want*, Crown of Life Ministries.

Collins, A., (2020), *The God Farm*, Crown of Life Ministries.

Collins, R., (2020), *My Journey with God: Traveling in the Supernatural Realm*, Crown of Life Ministries.

Kramer, J. P., (2020), *Where God Came Down*, Sourceflix.

Madden, P. J., (2015), *The Wigglesworth Standard*, Whitaker House.

Pittman, H., (1980), *Placebo*, scribd.com free PDF.

Ross, Dr. H., (2018), *The Creator and the Cosmos of God: How the Latest Scientific Discoveries reveal God* 4th Edition, RTB Press.

Ross, Dr. H., (2010), *Beyond the Cosmos: The Transdimensionality of God* 3rd Edition, RTB Press.

Tari, M., (1971), *Like a Mighty Wind*, Creation House.

Viloa, F. and Barna G., (2012), *Pagan Christianity,* Revised and Updated, Tyndale House.

Wallace, J. W., (2023), *Cold-Case Christianity: A Homicide Detective Investigates the Claims of the Gospel,* Updated and Expanded Edition, David C. Cook.

Wallace, J. W., (2016), *Cold-Case Christianity for Kids: Investigate Jesus with a Real Detective,* David C. Cook.

Woodworth-Etter, M., (1997), *Signs and Wonders*, Whittaker House.

Advanced Online Training

https://thegodfarm.com/

https://www.youtube.com/@thegodfarm514

www.ingramcontent.com/pod-product-compliance
Lightning Source LLC
Chambersburg PA
CBHW070536010526
44118CB00012B/1144